Cover Design by Lindsey Parks, Money Graphics LLC
Interior Layout by Matt Strieby, Newleaf Design
Author Photography by Steve White Films, Milwaukee, WI

ISBN: 978-0-9987208-0-7
LCCN: 2017902306

EVERYTHING WE TOUCH TURNS TO GOLD

A CANDID CONVERSATION WITH THE FLESH

KIMBERLY R. LOCK

TABLE OF CONTENTS

Prologue 7

The Flesh 13

Chapter 1: Humph! Don't You Shush Me! 15

Chapter 2: The Book of Life 30

Chapter 3: Who Do You Think You Are? 36

Chapter 4: Where Were You? 42

Chapter 5: Pause and Reflect 50

Chapter 6: Judgment vs. Discernment 53

Chapter 7: *The* Flesh vs. Your Flesh 57

The Spirit 65

Chapter 8: Shut Up! 67

Chapter 9: Who He Is 72

Chapter 10: Who I Am 77

Chapter 11: Who You Are 83

Chapter 12: Guilty as Charged 89

Chapter 13: Breathe Again 95

Chapter 14: When the Hurt and Healer Collide 98

Chapter 15: I Wanna Be Where You Are 103

Chapter 16: The Significance of Three 109

Chapter 17: My Shut-Up Moment 118

Epilogue 124

Acknowledgements 126

About Kimberly 127

PROLOGUE

Train up a child in the way he should go, and
when he is old he will not depart from it.

—Proverbs 22:6, NKJV

My mom and dad separated when I was four years old. As a result, my grandmother was instrumental in helping my mother teach me to have respect, dignity, and morals, not only as a woman, but also as a human being. My grandmother laid the spiritual foundation. She ensured that Jesus was a constant reality in our lives. I often slept over at "Granny's" (as we affectionately called her), while my mom worked multiple jobs to make ends meet. Granny loved Jesus, but she played no games. She raised 11 children (seven girls and four boys) in Bayou La Batre, Alabama, mostly alone, so she had to be strict. The children all ultimately migrated to Milwaukee, Wisconsin, and then relocated to various places across the U.S.

Granny was like Chinese food dipping sauce: sweet and spicy. She loved teaching her grands the principles of life that she had learned as a child. We were taught how to clean greens, string beans, wash clothes, clean chitterlings—you name it. On some weekends, when my other cousins and I would sleep over at Granny's house, we would get up early on Saturday mornings, travel with one of my aunts up north to farms where fresh vegetables were grown and available for picking and purchasing. We would pick greens, string beans, and strawberries. My aunt would make fresh strawberry cream cheese pies and punch bowl cakes with her pickings. We would then go back to Granny's place, where she would be making preparations for canning the greens and string beans. Granny always had cans and jars of something stored in the pantry or freezer bags in her deep freezer. If she used freezer bags, she would label the bags with the initial date they were frozen. Granny's wisdom for food storage was a very present help in times of hunger pangs. LOL.

✴ There are two things Granny loved: Jesus and her family. Bless her heart; she passed in 2014 at the age of 90. Please don't let the memories fool you though. Granny and her four-foot-and-some-inch frame played no games when it came to respect, especially when it involved teaching children how to have proper etiquette and to be respectful toward adults.

Some of the things I remember having instilled in me as a child include:

- Never call someone a lie.
- When someone gives you something, say, "Thank you."
- When asking for something, say, "May I please…"
- Do not interrupt someone when he or she is speaking.
- ✴ Treat people the way you want to be treated (but don't let nobody run over you). If I could use an emoji right here, I would be giving the side eye.
- Don't make fun of people.
- Ask for permission before doing anything.
- Pray. Don't ever forget to pray.
- When speaking to an adult, your reply to his or her statement should always be "Yes/no ma'am or sir."
- Hold your head up; always look a person in the eyes.
- Do not talk back.
- Do not say shut up.

And you better not call someone a lie! Ta HUH! No, what you meant to say was that person was telling a story. Calling someone a liar was like swearing.

The last statement on the list above was and still is a doozy. Shut up has a disrespectful and rude tone. It will immediately grasp your attention. Although we were taught to not tell someone else to shut up, Granny had no problem telling you to shut up. It didn't matter who you were. Young, old, male or female, adult or child. Mess around and try to explain yourself while she is talking! Get your mind right! Here it comes…

"Shut up! And I mean shut up rat na!"

With her commanding voice and stern look, all words immediately ceased. "Umm, Granny can I still breathe? Would the movement from my chest indicate to you that I am still trying to plead my cause or will you take the chest movement as a sign of me having life in my body?"

In the grand scheme of things, *shut up* was not all that bad. If she only said shut up, that was a good day. You got off easy, to some degree. Granny was not too ticked off. BUT…if Granny told you to *shut up* and then do something, like if there was an action that you must perform, after you cut off your voice from being heard, oh it just got real.

When *shut up* is accompanied with and *sit down*, you do not get to choose which one you would like to do. Okay. I dare you to get puffed up and sit down, but you kept talking or you kept talking but did not sit down. You will feel the presence of years of back-slapping experience with 11 children and wrinkles of hard labor from the back of her brown-toned hand grazing your lips so unexpectedly. The sheer quickness catches you off guard insomuch that you have no other choice, but to shut up…and sit! Granny had mastered the backhand and she was known to do it in church. If you were caught talking at any point during service, she will calmly walk out of the main sanctuary, just to catch you off guard and walk in undetected. You'll soon feel that anointed hand against your mouth…once again. BOP! "SHUT UP and I mean shut up rat na!"

No one ever thought to call CPS or anything. Shoot, they probably would have been backhanded, too. Don't be scared for us though. We all turned out pretty good. None of my cousins or myself had lifelong bruises or ever bled. No, we weren't abused. In fact, our upbringing kept us out of trouble with the law and helped us to learn what it meant to have integrity. Now that I think about it, I'm convinced that the grandmothers of old are absent from the lives of many youth today.

Although Granny's approach appeared brutal, she felt it was necessary to both get and retain our attention relative to important matters. It was serious for us as a family to understand what our beliefs were and what behavior was accepted as right or wrong. Neither did her approach make us question her love for us or make us love her any less. Sure, we went in the room and mumbled under our breath, but we would never disrespect Granny to her face.

In some instances, my grandmother was a lot like God, our Father. Have you ever gone through trials in life where it seemed as if you could not catch a break? If it isn't one thing, it's another. If not careful, you get to a point where you're thinking: *Why am I going through this?* The toughest situations bring us to our knees. It's almost like God has to place us in a position of brokenness, to finally sit still, fall into the hands of Jesus, and listen to Him. We often go through experiences because God knows how serious it is for His children to understand not only the schemes and plots of the enemy, but also to understand the love of God, our Father, which surpasses any thought or understanding that we have about what love really is. Some of those lessons have been self-imposed and some by spiritual design, but they all worked together for our good and His will. God has been molding and shaping us into the children He has always planned for us to be. However, our Father will not tolerate us being disrespectful toward Him. Sin is disrespect and rude. Sin is carried out through our fleshly desires, which are contrary to the principles that God, our Father, teaches. God has been using our life lessons to instill His spiritual morals, by way of His Son, Jesus Christ.

Just as there were consequences of not listening to my grandmother, so are there consequences of not being obedient to our Father. The key difference is that the consequences of disobedience to God will lead to death. That is why it is imperative that we are abrupt and to the point with ourselves. If you cannot be real with yourself, neither can you nor will you be with anyone else. We will go through life pretending to be someone or something we are not.

We need to literally tell the flesh to shut up and sit down. If not, then there are consequences:

- You cutoff your communication with your Father.
- You have no guidance and leadership that are mandatory in navigating through life's journey.
- You create separation, or enmity, between you and the kingdom of God.

Eventually, you'll attempt to justify ungodly behavior to a holy and perfect Father, which is the ultimate disrespect.

As a result, I present to you my narrative, intermingled with the precious word of God. I'd like to present it as a discussion. We are just having a heart-to-heart conversation about life. When I first joined the ministry my husband now oversees, his granddad (then pastor and founder) would say: "Thank you for coming. When you come, always bring your Bibles.

You never want someone to give you a message. Always ask them to show the Scripture." So, I'm bringing the word to you. I added biblical quotes that I reference because there may be someone who does not have access to the Bible at the time of reading. I just like to have proof of what I say, so that you can see it for yourselves.

> Eventually, you'll attempt to justify ungodly behavior to a holy and perfect Father, which is the ultimate disrespect.

By now, we should recognize that we only have one life. If we get it right, then all we need is one, but we must be cautious with who or what we allow to take up residence in our lives. Those relations can either fulfill or destroy us. I decided to write this book because I felt the need to speak in a language that is transparent and relatable. Please understand this. I did not write this book as an expert but to share my experiences that could hopefully help someone. I am subject to falling victim to my emotions, especially when someone prejudges my family or me without any basis for their opinion. But this one thing I do know: I believe and trust my Father. He presented me with a vivid depiction of judgment day over 18 years ago. That vision keeps me walking the straight and narrow. I have to talk to the flesh also. Honey, my flesh desires to go off, especially, when I know that I never take advantage of others and always consider them. When I am faced with a situation that will disappoint my Father and taint the character of my Savior, to whom I owe my existence, I almost always hear a voice that says, "It's all being written." Listen! I have NO TIME for hearing my Savior tell me, "I never knew you!" Ain't nobody got time for THAT (there's my side-eye again)! Later in this book, I will share the vision in hopes of it possibly helping you as well.

There seems to be a generational gap of people who were not taught to turn to Jesus for hope and guidance and thus they feel hopeless. I wanted to speak to a generation who may have not had a relationship with their grandmother as I did, who placed us on our knees beside her every night, as she would call out her children by name. Then, when she would get to the end, to make sure she covered everyone, she would say, "Bless them all, one by one and name by name." That would happen after she dozed off and then woke back up, still on her knees.

I wanted to speak to generations who do not truly understand the love that Jesus has for us because of the wickedness and disrespect for life itself that surrounds them or because they met an outlaw (not an in-law) to the throne of grace.

★ I wanted to speak to a generation that is scared and confused—scared to change and confused because those who say they are a representation of Jesus Christ seem to be just as lost.

★ I decided to write this book to let everyone know that the decisions you make are yours and the consequences of those decisions are yours as well.

I wrote this book to let everyone know that victory presented itself when super and natural collided. The omniscience of God, our Father, offered us with victory, when Jesus Christ was revealed in the flesh. Through the revelation of Jesus, we have the authority to tell the flesh to shut up and sit down and it must listen.

★ *Behold, I give you the authority to trample on serpents and scorpions, and over all the power of the enemy, and nothing shall by any means hurt you.* (Luke 10:19, NKJV)

SELF-PITY

REVENGE

JEALOUSY

GREED

INSENSITIVITY

HATRED

THE FLESH

MALICIOUSNESS

SELFISHNESS

HURT

ANGER

PRIDE

LUST

WORTHLESSNESS

UNFORGIVING

LONELINESS

Humph! Don't You Shush Me!

"Don't shush me! I'll make all the noise I wanna!"

—DAFFY DUCK

Growing up, I could not wait until Saturday morning, to watch the lineup of cartoon shows. One of my favorites was *Looney Tunes*, particularly Bugs Bunny. He and his feud between Elmer Fudd and Daffy Duck were unmatched. Daffy was always trying to prove that he was just as good as Bugs, but someone would be on the short end of the stick—hurt, burnt up, and humiliated. One episode, Daffy was at Porky Pig's house with Porky's dog. The dog tried to prevent Daffy from leaving. Daffy is notoriously loud and so the dog tells him to "shush." What does Daffy do? Of course, he is stubborn and over the top. Sounds like our flesh, right? When we try to calm it down, it only becomes more boisterous. There is a reason why and we will get into it now.

Let's begin our discussion with a review of the book title. Of course, I wanted a title that would capture your attention, but it was more than just a title for me. The title of this book came about through my cousin Kara. About two years ago, she came to me and said the Lord had placed on her heart a book title for me. It immediately caught my attention; however, I was trying to complete a children's series that started as a self-publication, to a published, to a temporary shelved series. With all I had to think about with this monkey children's series, (well, that is how I felt with the back and forth of this here stuff), I did not give the book that you are reading right now one bit of a thought.

In November 2016, the title crossed my mind and I thought, *Okay Lord, should I be doing something with this?* I sat down and immediately an outline and structure of the manuscript came to mind along with key points that I needed to focus on. I reached out to Kara (whom I call SCF: Sister, Cousin, Friend), expressed my gratitude, and told her the book was coming to fruition. As you could imagine, she was ecstatic and so was I. What would I do with my children's series, Lord? I pondered. This new book pressed on me heavily. It was not that the children's books weren't completed. They are; they just haven't been completely produced. But this book right here, the one that you are now holding, had a sense of urgency behind it. As I wrote, I was uncertain of why I had to move quickly, but I am always sensitive to the Spirit and what He demands so that His purpose can be fulfilled in my life, which ultimately leads me to fulfilling my purpose.

> **The intent isn't to be offensive but rather draw you to the sense of urgency that is needed before the flesh attempts to take ownership of something or someone it does not own...you!**

The Bible states in Proverbs 4:7 that getting wisdom is the wisest thing we can do, and before anything else, we should get an understanding. Therefore, I will provide a clearer understanding of why it is necessary to *shut up* AND *sit down* by breaking down the title of this book. The intent isn't to be offensive but rather to draw you to the sense of urgency that is needed before the flesh attempts to take ownership of something or someone it does not own...you! The implications of *shut up* is to be abrupt and deliberate enough for us to truly grasp the war between the flesh and spirit.

Shut up is intentional and direct. The use of it in any conversation is just flat-out rude, but it commands the room and demands immediate action. I suppose a nicer tone or better understanding of what it means to shut up and sit down is to pause and reflect, but I'm not trying to be nice or pacify anyone. We have been pacified far too long and have made provisions and justifications for our own actions, which have separated us so far from God and the truth that we begin to believe the nonsense that comes from our mouths. Enough is enough. Let's get right into it.

SHUT UP
"How rude..."
—Stephanie Tanner, *Full House*

Have you ever tried to read a book at Chuck E. Cheese's? Why not? When you need to prepare for an exam, would you go to an amusement park? Probably not, at least not intentionally. When you become a parent with more than one child, you learn how to multitask and do what is needed. Other than the obvious, why wouldn't you intentionally study at Chuck E. Cheese or Six Flags? There are just too many distractions and it is too noisy. Would you visit a day spa that is in the midst of a childcare center? Uhhh nooo! I'm trying to have a brief "whoosah" moment away from my children and not with anyone else's. Ahh, it makes sense then why spas and libraries seek locations and structures to support peace and tranquility that would allow guests the ability to relax or mentally focus.

There's power in silence. We can hear the Spirit of the Lord speaking to us in quiet places.

Why do we need to tell the flesh to *shut up?* The phrase is an intrusion, forcibly taking over any situation or conversation. We need to tell the flesh to stop and command it to forcibly do so. By doing this, we are taking away the fleshly desires ability to be in control. Can I help you with something? We cannot make our flesh live holy. Sounds crazy, right? Well, we cannot, because the flesh cannot please God.

> **There's power in silence. We can hear the Spirit of the Lord speaking to us in quiet places.**

For those who live according to the flesh set their minds on the things of the flesh, but those who live according to the Spirit, the things of the Spirit. For to be carnally minded is death, but to be spiritually minded is life and peace. Because the carnal mind is enmity against God; for it is not subject to the law of God, nor indeed can be. So then, those who are in the flesh cannot please God. (Romans 8:5-8, NKJV)

The flesh cannot fight a spiritual battle. Therefore, we must stop approaching the battles of life as if we can do this ourselves. Verse 7 says our carnal mind is an enmity (enemy) against God. Our own mind creates

> **The flesh cannot fight a spiritual battle. Therefore, we must stop approaching the battles of life as if we can do this ourselves.**

hostility between God and us because it cannot submit to the law of God.

For example, you and the team you work with decide to meet after work at a restaurant that also has a bar. Maybe you are celebrating the completion of a successful implementation or maybe you all have decided to de-stress from an ongoing issue and just meet outside the walls of the company. Or, maybe you overheard some team members talking about just getting together and you decide to join them for a few hours. Your mind will tell you that it is okay to sociably drink just if it is not in excess, and plus, the Bible say that wine is good for the stomach's sake (I would definitely insert a side-eye meme here if I had one). However, we know that having a "few" drinks destroys our ability to think clearly and logically. The Bible may speak on wine, but it also says do not be offensive in anything.

We give no offense in anything, that our ministry may not be blamed. (2 Corinthians 6:3, NKJV)

Your life and how you live it, is a ministry to others.

Let us continue with this illustration. Perhaps on this day that you are hanging out, a new convert from the church happens to be at the same restaurant and sees you turning one back. Would you even have a conscience at that point to explain? Would your mind conjure up what you could say? Would you pretend as if you did not see this person? Would you make the situation comical and blame someone else? Just the appearance of you being in this setting should seem awkward. Think about this: what if your explanation leads the individual to feel that drinking is justifiable as followers of Jesus and when the opportunity presents itself, maybe in a different setting or a different day, he or she recalls your words and has a few drinks? However, the story for the new convert ends slightly different. After giving an occasion to the flesh to stumble, this person drives home and has an accident and does not make it. Seems far-fetched to you? It is not. Your life is that important to give you the real.

Oh, okay, here is another thought: after all that I have read and studied about Jesus, I have an image of Him being pure and holy. He would never have a thought of yielding to sin. Worthy is the Lamb of God, who was slain for the sins of the world—my Savior. But if I saw Jesus having a drink? My Savior? The One who I said pulled me from a dying situation and gave me life? Ohhhh my meme right here would be one of "Uh, excuse me Jesus." Awkward! "Ummm" (clears throat) "excuse me, Jesus, but, ummm, this doesn't feel right. Are you still pure having this drink? How does Your Father feel about this? I know You can relate to us and You were tempted as we are, but since when did You begin giving into temptation? Jesus, this ain't even You. I thought the wine You talked about was not the wine we drink today that gets us all drunk. Jesus, wait! I'll make a way for You to escape—this is wrong. Let me get You out of here. I cannot let You do this, Jesus."

Right? That is the response I would have. It would just feel weird. Well, the Spirit of the Living God, who has power over the flesh, should be a strong conviction for you to stand up and say, "Uh-uh, this just seems wrong."

For we do not have a High Priest who cannot sympathize with our weaknesses, but was in all points tempted as we are, yet without sin. (Hebrews 4:15, NKJV)

Flesh Assessment:
1. What is your flesh saying without you opening your mouth? You, see, your physical disposition is a voice and produces a strength that you may not recognize. Your eyes can let a person know if you are approachable or do not feel like being bothered today.

I went on a field trip with my then 10-year-old daughter. The field trip provided exhibits of how people would communicate back in the day through technology, clothing that was worn, family games, and pastime activities. They also gave examples of ways in which women would flirt in the saloon to show a man her interest. A certain way she would position her fan would indicate if she accepted the man's advances or if she was married. A bat of the eyes or a bit of leg exposure could tell what type of woman the man was dealing with.

2. What signs are your flesh giving that speak contrary to the words of God?

It is time to take away the voice of the flesh, which would ultimately take away power and control.

> *A time to tear and a time to mend. A time to be quiet and a time to speak.* (Ecclesiastes 3:7, NLT)

AND
"So…And?"

How many times have you used the word *and* in a sentence? I'm sure probably more than you can even imagine. Without consideration, we use this word every day, but have we paid attention to how much power and significance it produces? When I was in school, we learned early the use of conjunction words. I am still in school, helping all of my children with their homework (side-eye meme again). What I found is that this lesson is still included in the teacher's English guidelines. A conjunction is defined as two or more events occurring at the same time. In other words, conjunctions are the glue that holds the sentences we make together. Some other examples of conjunction words include because, but, and when. See—I just used *and* in the last sentence. Anyway, the use of *and* is going to reiterate how serious we are about shutting down the flesh. We need *and* to bring together two events: *shut up, sit down*. The word *and* is going to let the flesh know who is really in control. *And* is going to reiterate the control that the Spirit of God commands over the flesh.

Jesus brought attention to two events occurring at the same time through the use of *and* so that we clearly understand who He is, the relationship between Him, His Father, and the spiritual structure of the kingdom of God:

> *Jesus said to him, "I am the way, the truth, and the life. No one comes to the Father except through Me."* (John 14:6, NKJV)

C'mon here, Jesus. Not only is He the way to the Father, Jesus is the truth, which is the opposite of who the enemy is, the father of lies (John 8:44), *AND* Jesus is the life. Jesus is the bread of life (John 6:35). What happens if you do not eat? You become malnourished and could ultimately die. Jesus is the bread of life. Without Him, we die a spiritual death that lasts for eternity.

Have you come to a point in your life where you have misused the conjunction *and* incorrectly by connecting events that produced fleshly and spiritual conflict?

It's time to disconnect and reconnect to the Way, Truth, *and* Life!

SIT DOWN

"Tell the negative committee that sits inside your head to sit down and shut up."
—ANN BRADFORD

Why is sitting so critical?

I think my husband and I have tried just about all of the latest workout DVD systems, especially the Beachbody brand. P90X, P90X Plus, P90X3, 21 Day Fix, Body Beast—I could go on and on. Regardless of what program you are on, whether homemade or developed specific to your needs, at the end of the workout, there is a cool down phase. Most workout regimes request you do not skip the cool down phase. Cooling down allows your breath to stabilize and your heart rate to decrease, which then creates a calming effect. Sitting also calms down your brain so you can focus. When we are calm, we rationalize our feelings and emotions. We are able to recall to our mind what the word of God says. We can remember that for every reaction, there is an action and that action has a consequence.

> **The purpose of the seat is for you to rise up better than when you went down.**

When you are sitting, you are required to remain in a temporary position, to focus on what is in front of you. If you think about physically sitting, you are in a lower place than normal. The purpose of the seat is for you to rise up better than when you went down. So, have several of them and take your time getting up. Make a deliberate effort to rise up better than you were before. Oh, see, I will go there. I'm going there...THIS I recall to my mind, therefore I have hope, it is of the Lord's mercies that we are not consumed. His compassions do not fail. Oh Father, great is Your faithfulness—see right there, all I did was remember the words of the Lord, which brought me back to where I needed to be:

This I recall to my mind, therefore I have hope. Through the Lord's mercies we are not consumed, because His compassions fail not. They are new every morning; Great is Your faithfulness. (Lamentations 3:21-23, NKJV)

Because God is faithful, I will remain faithful to Him in conducting myself with integrity to carry out the family business—kingdom business.

I have a question: If Jesus was sitting right next to you, would you still ponder the temptation that is driving you or would you ask Him to help you? Oddly enough, He is next to you. He is right there waiting for you to confess and ask for His help.

✝ *For with the heart one believes unto righteousness, and with the mouth confession is made unto salvation.* (Romans 10:10, NKJV)

With our heart, we believe that we can be in right standing with God. Confession is done to present you with the gift of salvation, which is given through Jesus Christ. Salvation is the deliverance from the power of sin. Having one confess is the acknowledgement that Jesus Christ is Lord and that you need help with whatever issue. You are simply telling Jesus that whatever you are dealing with, you cannot deal with it on your own and that you have come to the realization that you need Jesus and that you need Him now! Why confess with your mouth? Honey, whatever is in your heart will eventually come out of your mouth, but it must be in your heart first.

The Bible tells us in Mark 7:18-22 that it isn't what we put in us that defiles us or makes us corrupt because it does not enter our heart. What corrupts us enters our heart and is then outwardly displayed. We need an internal makeover, a spiritual detox. Once we change what is in our heart, make no mistake, the change will show up on the outside.

Flesh Assessment:
1. What mistakes have you made and are you on the path to repeat them?
2. Is it time for you to have a seat?

CANDID
"Smile, you're on Candid Camera!"

A candid discussion means that you are sincere. You have let your guard down and you have shared your innermost emotions. Psychologists are great with creating a safe place for a person to feel comfortable enough to open up. Being open and honest with yourself may be one of the most challenging things to do, because it requires you to be accountable for your own behavior. That behavior results in accountability to God.

So then each of us shall give account of himself to God. (Romans 14:12, NKJV)

Just as a psychologist can provide a physical location that harbors feelings of safety and comfort, there should be a place where you can physically and mentally disconnect from the pressures

> **To grow yourself, you must be able to reflect on who you are and where you are.**

of life and focus on what is important. To grow yourself, you must be able to reflect on who you are and where you are. Now that I am aware of myself because I have calmed down, I can step outside of myself and reflect.

- We live in a society where we must personify perfection.
- We wear makeup to cover the flaws in our skin, which gives the appearance of flawlessness.
- We wear girdles and waist trainers to give the appearance of the perfect physical shape.
- We wear high heels to give the appearance of confidence, beauty, and class.

We take countless pictures with our camera phones to capture the perfect pose to post on social media. For what? All of this is for what? Most would reply to this question by saying it is because they want to, but consider this: you saw someone else doing these things and thought it was cute. Mmmm hmmm. I know when I saw my momma put on her heels, as a child I would go in her closet and pick out the shoes that I said would be mine when I would get older. I would then ask if she would keep them so I could wear them. When Momma wore heels with her dress, she looked confident. Her legs looked more toned and lean. She just looked good! You saw someone do something and their appearance influenced you, insomuch that you decided to try out these ideals yourself, thinking it would lead to a better you or a better representation of you.

The changes described are temporal. When I take off my platform wedges, I am still five-feet-six-inches tall, take it or leave it. When I unwrap that girdle from around my waist, sucking in the pounds acquired from being pregnant five times, everything falls back to its original shape. Honey, when I take off the eyeliner, my eyes return to their natural puffy state. We do all this for a better representation of ourselves, but what have we done to our spirit to give a better representation of Jesus?

Flesh Assessment:

1. Is there a physical location that you can go to to let your guard down? Just you and the Lord?
2. Get there and visit that place often. If you are looking for someone you can just be real with and be yourself, I know no better candidate that God, because He made you. He knows all about you anyway. In fact, He can tell you some things about yourself, that you have yet to realize. Let His light shine through you and not your own.

Let your light so shine before men, that they may see your good works and glorify your Father in heaven. (Matthew 5:16, NKJV)

CONVERSATION
"Come and Talk to Me, I Really Wanna Know You"
—JODECI

There are many ways to communicate. For example, we communicate via social media, facial expressions, body language, and eye contact. If email is a form of communication on your job, this may be one of the first tasks you complete once you arrive. You sit down, check your email, and your manager or supervisor has sent a team communication regarding a status update on an issue. That is a form of communication. Two computers networked together can communicate. Communication can occur with no exchange of information. However, when I am having a conversation, there is some exchange going on.

When someone is having a conversation, it is meant to be an exchange of ideas and thoughts that produces information for the recipient. Let me say it like this: I have a relationship with my Father, God. When I go to Him in prayer, I am conversing with Him through the Holy Spirit. I am transferring my emotions, thoughts, and feelings to produce an action or a reaction. In other words, I expect a move. Bae bae, when I converse with my Savior, it is not always me asking, but mainly me letting Him know that I know that He is good, He is in control, and that I humble myself before Him. I recognize that I am nothing without Him. I let Jesus know that I respect Him and even when life happens and I am hurt to the core, He is still in control and has my best interest at heart.

Back in the 1990s there was a popular R&B group named Jodeci. They created a song that became popular titled "Come and Talk to Me." I could imagine the Lord, making the same statement: you talk to everyone else… come and talk to Me.

Flesh Assessment:
Try this communication activity. Jot down your answers. If you are uncertain of the answer, it is time for a real conversation between you and Jesus.

1. How do you know that you'll go to heaven when you die?
2. How are you growing personally?
3. In a conversation with someone who has never heard about God, what would you say about Him from your experience?
4. Does your representation of Jesus reflect the experience? Would the person you are speaking with desire to know Jesus as his or her personal Savior or continue to live without Him?

WITH THE FLESH
"Wax off, wax on!"
—THE KARATE KID

✈You are with you all day every day. You cannot get a break from you. No matter where you go, you are always there. Let's say you are tired of your job/current position and you decide to apply for another job/position. If you have not put forth any effort to improve yourself, to grow and increase in knowledge, you will ultimately end up with the same results, same complaints, and same problems you experienced with the previous job. Why? Because you are the same person. You are seeking fulfillment with minimal to no effort of knowing yourself and growing yourself.

The entire point of this is really simple. The conversation with the flesh is for you to begin to listen to the heart of whom we are talking with, which

> **The conversation with the flesh is for you to begin to listen to the heart of whom we are talking with, which will then reveal who we really are (or who we need to become) in Jesus Christ.**

will then reveal who we really are (or who we need to become) in Jesus Christ. I have intentionally stated "the" flesh and not "your" flesh in most cases up until this point because there is a major contrast of which I will explain in the next chapter. Your flesh causes you to become subject to "the flesh."

There are major consequences with trying to live a spiritual life in the flesh. You will experience inward and outward struggles that will ultimately lead to spiritual fatigue and failure. If we could win this life in the flesh, why would God tell us this?

> *For the weapons of our warfare are not carnal but mighty in God for pulling down strongholds, casting down arguments and every high thing that exalts itself against the knowledge of God, bringing every thought into captivity to the obedience of Christ.* (2 Corinthians 10:4-5, NKJV)

If we continue to attempt to enter the battle unequipped, we set ourselves up to become spiritual dropouts. The Bible says it like this:

> **If we continue to attempt to enter the battle unequipped, we set ourselves up to become spiritual dropouts.**

> *Having a form of godliness but denying its power. And from such people turn away!* (2 Timothy 3:5, NKJV)

You will act religious but reject the power of God that could make you spiritual. If you do not spiritually drop out, you will become a floater going from church to church. For a moment, you are fulfilled because it is a body of believers who may conduct things differently than what you have been accustom to. Your flesh is excited, but then as time goes on, you then realize that this new ministry is also a hospital for the spiritually dead. The root of the matter is the seed has not taken root and you are seeking spiritual gratification with a carnal perception.

In the original *The Karate Kid*, Daniel was taught to clean and wax his karate master's car, or so it appeared on the surface. But Mr. Miyagi was teaching a specific movement that was critical to Daniel's training. We can learn from this. Wax off the old deeds of your flesh, and wax on the spirit man that requires a renewed mind and living in true righteousness and holiness, according to the word of God.

> *...that you put off, concerning your former conduct, the old man which grows corrupt according to the deceitful lusts, and be renewed in the spirit of your mind, and that you put on the new man which was created according to God, in true righteousness and holiness.* (Ephesians 4:22-24, NKJV)

Flesh Assessment:
1. How are you going to overcome the flesh?
2. Will you continue to make provisions?
3. Have you taken off the old "man" and put on the new? The old man is the flesh because you have become a new creature in Christ (2 Corinthians 5:17); the old man and the old things the old man used to do are supposed to be done away with—cast aside and left alone.

The Book of Life

*And I saw the dead, small and great, standing
before God, and books were opened. And another
book was opened, which is the Book of Life. And
the dead were judged according to their works, by
the things which were written in the books.*

—Revelation 20:12, NKJV

What makes a book worth reading to you? Maybe the drama. Maybe it's on a subject you want to learn about. Maybe most of your books consist of images and a few words, because you are at a point in your life of teaching some little one the importance of reading and the world of imagination that unfolds in a book. Maybe you saw a movie that was based upon a best-selling novel, which prompted you to purchase the book. Whatever tickles your fancy, we should always take the time to step away from our technological gadgets and social media and allow our minds the opportunity to continue to grow and expand through literature.

The general format or layout of most books begins with a section called the foreword. The foreword is usually written by someone other than the author, providing his/her opinion about the book and a little insight into the author. Following the foreword, a book contains an introduction, chapters, a conclusion, acknowledgements, and references to other resources the author may have mentioned while writing.

Think about your life right now and where the journey began. We are all authors. Our lives are like a book with many chapters. We began our manuscript with co-authors, our parents, because we were too young to begin this process alone. We were newbies in this industry and needed the assistance of some people who had knowledge and understanding. The authors were further along in the process to assist us with navigating. Although they were still learning, they were not babes as we were.

A child grows physically and increases in knowledge, ultimately becoming THE contributor but with key influences. There were many days of edits, reviews, deletions, additions, and further explanations to a topic all pertaining to the subject of life. Each day is a new page and each year is a new chapter. Let's review the layout of *the book of life*. The manuscript of life becomes a book when someone else can learn from your journey. Let us look at life's novel more closely.

The foreword begins with a nine-month journey in the womb written by God, our Father.

> *"Before I formed you in the womb I knew you; Before you were born I sanctified you; I ordained you a prophet to the nations."* (Jeremiah 1:5, NKJV

The introduction is when we are physically born (introduced) to our parents. They are assigned as the co-authors of our book.

> *Children, obey your parents in the Lord, for this is right. Honor your father and mother, which is the first commandment with promise: that it may be well with you and you may live long on the earth. And you, fathers, do not provoke your children to wrath, but bring them up in the training and admonition of the Lord.* (Ephesians 6:1-4, NKJV)

Then, the chapters of life begin. As with any good read, our lives consist of successes, triumphs, and tragedies. Characters are introduced. Some remain throughout our entire life story and some are there for a season. Some were never meant to stay as long as they did. In fact, some were never a part of the plot at all, and yet they still served a purpose.

> *And we know that all things work together for good to those who love God, to those who are the called according to His purpose.* (Romans 8:28, NKJV)

Since it all works out in the end anyway, I have decided that my life's book will be a best-seller. How do we become best-sellers of our own story?

- A best-seller in life is a victor and not a victim.
- A best-seller in life turns tragedy into triumphs.
- A best-seller in life realizes that their sufficiency is in Jesus.
- A best-seller in life comes running back to his/her Father through Jesus Christ, like the prodigal son.
- A best-seller in life is not selfish. He or she uses his/her own book to help create a best-seller for someone else.

Don't copy and paste the same page in a new chapter because you are then plagiarizing your own life. Stop erasing and rewriting the same story with new characters. If you do, your book will never reach its fullest potential. You cannot begin a new chapter by repeating the same page. I don't sit here as a person who pretends as if I know how to balance it all. I sit here flawed. I yell at my children. I get frustrated quite often when they do a horrible job at completing their chores. I don't always respond to "the tap on the shoulder" with a Coke and a smile (that is the G-rated version to the intimacy call by the husband—here goes my "eyes wide open" emoji right here). Bae baee, there is some grumbling and frustration going on, especially when I am sleeping well.

> **Don't copy and paste the same page in a new chapter because you are then plagiarizing your own life.** *to take ideas or writing for another and pass them off as ones own*

What I have decided to do is acknowledge the Lord in everything. I came to the realization that early in my life, my God was there. Jesus had sent angels to cover me in circumstances that could have been tragic for me. If He looked out for me when I did not have a lick of sense, why wouldn't I seek Him for help now that I have entered a relationship with Him? Listen people. Just because the Lord does not give us what we want does not mean He is not good. I have to digress for a moment.

Why do we place the almighty God in a box? We have redefined the term provider to mean "Lord, when I ask for it, You give it to me." Really? Like that does not happen in THIS world, with anyone we identified as a caretaker. Let us have that same condescending tone and attitude toward our mothers or fathers—talk about *shut up* and *sit down*? You better run! In fact, I hope you had an apartment with the first month's rent already taken care of and keys in hand. So, if our earthly parents have standards, c'mon, you think the Creator of all is going to bow down to our demands? You must be speaking to an idol god, not God, my Father. Mmm Mmmm

Condescend - to be gracious about doing a thing regarded as beneath one's dignity. Deal with other in a proud & haughty

noooo no no no no. Somebody dun told you wrong. Please tell the flesh to find the largest stadium ever built, *shut up*, and have several seats!

In 2017, I intentionally began restructuring my book of life. It is called, *The Year of My Father's Business: The Powerful and Humbling Story of a Daughter and the Power Her Father Gave Her to Operate His Business!* I don't know how many chapters I have remaining in my book, but I do know this: The remaining chapters will be better than the beginning because my Father didn't just tell me, He made me a promise.

The glory of this latter temple shall be greater than the former,' says the Lord of hosts. 'And in this place I will give peace,' says the Lord of hosts. (Haggai 2:9, NKJV)

This house (my body) is where the Spirit of God rests comfortably because I make sure He feels right at home.

I beseech you therefore, brethren, by the mercies of God, that you present your bodies a living sacrifice, holy, acceptable to God, which is your reasonable service. (Romans 12:1, NKJV)

As far as the conclusion goes, if I am not confident of anything else, I do know that my conclusion will be breathtaking and my book will be found on Heaven's best-seller's list: The Book of Life.

Then I saw a new heaven and a new earth, for the old heaven and the old earth had disappeared. And the sea was also gone. I heard a loud shout from the throne, saying, "Look, God's home is now among his people! He will live with them, and they will be his people. God himself will be with them. He will wipe every tear from their eyes, and there will be no more death or sorrow or crying or pain. All these things are gone forever. (Revelation 21:1; 3-4, NLT)

Flesh Assessment:
1. Everything we do and say is being written in the eternal book of life. The Holy Spirit sits as a court stenographer, documenting every action and behavior as a witness to the accountability that we must give when we stand before the Lord. Because you are a "published author," how are you writing your story?

2. Are you writing with expectation?
3. Is there some structure? Are you writing with integrity and wisdom, where possibly your book could be used as a reference Tool for someone who has begun writing?
4. Are you seeking guidance from the Holy Spirit, who is the master editor and can assist you creating a best-seller?

NOTES CHAPTER 2

Who Do You Think You Are?

"Mister big stuff, who do you think you are?"

—JEAN KNIGHT

I remember that song—Jean Knight. I grew up, as most of us, in a family where music was a part of our lives. I love the old R&B songs.

As businesses form, they develop guidelines for operations that lay the foundation for who the business is and what it represents. In almost every aspect of our lives, there are stipulations, codes, and guidelines that correspond to the affiliation with an organization and support the organizational structure. Most companies also develop what is called a code of conduct or code of ethics. These documents provide information on how employees should conduct themselves as representatives of the organization. It may also include dress codes (formal or informal); the company's mission, vision, values, objectives; and how employees should address (ethical) situations.

Not only does corporate America have rules, but also colleges have entrance requirements. The most prestigious of them all seek potential students who strive for excellence. Proof of their perseverance would be demonstrated through the applicants' overall grade point average, test scores on the SAT or ACT, and how well they have written their entrance essay, along with any recommendation letters from reliable sources.

Athletic teams from all levels also have requirements. For high school, a student's GPA and behavior in class coupled with work ethic may get him or her a spot on the team. For college recruitment, one may have been scouted based on four years of performance during high school to land a sweet spot in a starting position.

Seeing then that the word in every facet of life and entity has some sort of structure for conducting business and extracurricular activities, why is it that when we give our lives to the Lord, we feel as if there should be no ethical standard for us to fulfill and uphold? While we may not verbalize this theory, our actions are loud and clear.

We wear our shirt as low as we want (cleavage showing).
We wear our skirts as tight and short as we like.
We wear our pants as tight as we want.
Men wear earrings because of they like how it looks.
We get piercings everywhere we desire.
We go where we want.
We do what we want.
We say what we want and how we want.

I'm not speaking of the lifestyle we lived before meeting the Lord. I am speaking of representation after saying we have surrendered all to our blessed Savior, Jesus. If we are doing everything WE want, then who are we really representing?

If you do what you want to do, then you are representing you. If we do not acknowledge the Holy Spirit in all that we do, we are representing the flesh.

But put on the Lord Jesus Christ, and make no provision for the flesh, to fulfill its lusts. (Romans 13:14, NKJV)

> **If we are doing everything WE want, then who are we really representing?**

We put on everything else, but have we yet put on Christ? Am I saying that your attire is going to determine where you spend eternity? No, of course not. God judges our heart, our faith, and our willingness to be a living sacrifice. But it seems that we are so busy trying to relate to the world that we have begun confirming and not transforming the minds. If the list of things I have mentioned brings attention to you and not the Spirit of God dwelling in you, then you are operating in the flesh.

The ultimate power of persuasion was demonstrated through Jesus. Think about how you were persuaded to repent and change from your own ways. If you grew up in church as I did, most times you did not want to go and when you did, you turned a deaf ear. You became immune to the word of God and it resonated in you as tradition: something we had to do. It was not until you were in a seated position, looking for a way to stand up again, that the Lord Jesus sent a true vessel your way and your ears became open to the truth. That person spoke with love and comfort. They did not try to preach hell out of you. They shared with you their struggles—what they had done in life and even what they still were facing. But they also gave you hope. They told you how they manage to navigate through life and where their strength lies, which is in Jesus Christ.

The power of persuasion is demonstrated through love.

> *The Lord has appeared of old to me, saying: Yes, I have loved you with an everlasting love; therefore, with lovingkindness I have drawn you.* (Jeremiah 31:3, NKJV)

Everything God has ever done was of quality and excellence. With God as our Father, and we as His children, we should be the epitome of class, sprinkled with grace, and topped off with a silent confidence that only comes from the peace and joy given to us by our Father, through our Savior, Jesus Christ.

> *Let your speech always be with grace, seasoned with salt, that you may know how you ought to answer each one.* (Colossians 4:6, NKJV)

Do you really know who you are? You are chosen and to be chosen means to be the object of choice or divine favor.

> *You did not choose Me, but I chose you and appointed you that you should go and bear fruit, and that your fruit should remain, that whatever you ask the Father in My name He may give you.* (John 15:16, NKJV)

You were chosen because you are considered the "cream of the crop" to represent Jesus.

You were selected from all the other billions of candidates to show forth the praises of our Savior. There was no other person created to do what you do, because the Master Designer, God our Father, specifically made you for a purpose. God has all the confidence in you, but you choose to represent the flesh and do what it pleases, regardless of who it offends. Because of your selfishness, that one soul or the masses of souls our Savior needs you to connect with because of the power in your testimony, remain lost in their sin longer than intended. And so, just as the

> **You are chosen and to be chosen means to be the object of choice or divine favor.**

children of Israel who wandered for forty years, these people continue to wander, all because your representation is unclear.

If someone rings your doorbell and says he or she is with Fed-Ex or UPS and has a package for you, what are you going to look for? Well, first I need to see a truck with the official brand name. Next, I need to see the delivery person with a shirt that also matches the official brand on the truck. Then, I need to see a package on the ground and a gadget in the delivery person's hand for me to sign. I am going to make sure the delivery person really is a representative of the company.

Is your representation clear of whom you say you are? If you are a child of the Most High God, you need to conduct and carry yourself as such. Let me make it more plain: in case you were unaware, you are chosen. You are royalty. We have been commissioned to earth to show forth the majesty of the kingdom of God that awaits all of us who turn from our own malicious ways to follow the example that Jesus laid before us. The mission is to compel the wandering souls. Let us represent the kingdom of God, our Father, as heirs to the throne.

> *But you are a chosen generation, a royal priesthood, a holy nation,*
> *His own special people, that you may proclaim the praises of Him who*
> *called you out of darkness into His marvelous light.* (1 Peter 2:9, NKJV)

The next time someone asks, "Who do you think you are?" tell him or her you are royalty. Let us be clear though. You cannot receive the riches of the kingdom that your Father owns if you continue to operate in the flesh because it is an enemy against your Father. The mark of royalty is what one is born into and has nothing to do with ability or merit.

Flesh Assessment:
1. Have you neglected the call to royalty?
2. Do you stand with the crowd or taller than the crowd? Not in a prideful or boastful manner, but as one who can help those who are unable to move from their seated position without assistance. But of course, you cannot help if you are seated as well. You are a carrier of the heavenly delivery services, on assignment, to reintroduce life.

Tell your flesh to shut up and sit down. It's time to get to work!

Where Were You?

"Scooby Doo, where are you?"

—HANNA-BARBERA PRODUCTIONS

esus walked this earth and felt as we feel about many situations. That is why He is the ultimate sacrifice and He can relate to our lives and feelings.

Seeing then that we have a great High Priest who has passed through the heavens, Jesus the Son of God, let us hold fast our confession. For we do not have a High Priest who cannot sympathize with our weaknesses, but was in all points tempted as we are, yet without sin. Hebrews 4:14-15, NKJV)

In John 11, we are able to witness some of the human emotions of Jesus. His friend, Lazarus, became ill. Lazarus had two sisters, Martha and Mary. This is the same Martha who washed the feet of Jesus with her hair. Martha is the same one who got mad at Mary when Jesus came to her house, because Mary wasn't helping out in the kitchen with the food (I'm paraphrasing) in Luke 10.

The Bible declares that Jesus loved Lazarus and his sisters. Not long after being ill for some time, Lazarus died. The Bible says that Jesus wept and those in their company cried along with Jesus. Mary got emotional though. Almost as if she was going off on Jesus, she fell to His feet. She goes on to tell Jesus if He had been there, her brother would not have died.

How many times have you blamed the Lord for bad situations in your life? How often have we gotten an "attitude" with God because the situation was not as favorable as we would have hoped? Or God didn't do what we wanted Him to do?

The Lord is not to blame for the tragedies and hardships in our lives. It seems as if this is hard for us to believe. He told us who is behind all of this.

The thief does not come except to steal, and to kill, and to destroy. I have come that they may have life, and that they may have it more abundantly. (John 10:10, NKJV)

Now, I don't take an abundant life to mean there won't be problems. No, that is a false sense of reality. If you research any well-known person, you learn of the magnitude of their struggles and how they persevered because of their purpose. Fulfilling that purpose led to an abundant life.

So, how is it that this chosen generation, selected to be royalty, can be so quick to question the integrity of the Lord, His decisions, and His whereabouts in their lives? While you are in the flesh and sitting down, consider that there just may be some questions the Lord has of you as He did of Job.

Who is this who darkens counsel by words without knowledge? Now prepare yourself like a man; I will question you, and you shall answer Me. Where were you when I laid the foundations of the earth? Tell Me, if you have understanding? (Job 38:2-4, NKJV)

We seek pleasure.
We seek fulfillment.
We seek to escape from pain.
Do we seek God? Yeah, we do. In some respect. Here is how we seek Him:

Ask, and it will be given to you; seek, and you will find; knock, and it will be opened to you. (Matthew 7:7, NKJV)

This Scripture has taken on a meaning of its own in the church realm. If we assume that "ask and you will receive" means "ask for anything you want and I'll give it to you," then we have turned the Lord into a genie in a bottle who anxiously awaits the next request from our laundry list of wishes. Some people are led to believe that this Scripture implies we can ask for that house, car, spouse, dog, or cat and the Lord will move. If that is the case, the Scripture above is contradictory to this and the one thing God is not is the author of confusion.

> But seek first the kingdom of God and His righteousness, and all these things shall be added to you. (Matthew 6:33, NKJV)

Why would Jesus tell us in this Scripture to seek the Kingdom of God and He will add the things, if all we were obligated to do was ask, seek, and knock? See the blessing is not the house, the car, the spouse, the dog. Those are things. The blessing is the open door the Lord placed before you, that no man could shut for you to get the house…the car…the spouse… the dog! The blessing is how your credit score was not high enough to get the vehicle, but then the salesman pulled out dealership incentives and bonuses to make the payments affordable and for you to leave the lot with the new vehicle. Now, that is a blessing! People who steal clothes have nice clothes, because they stole them—hello somebody. The question is what are you seeking first?

We seek backwards. We enter a bargaining agreement with the Lord that is completely opposite of this Scripture: "Lord, if You give me a husband, I will be faithful to You. We will read together, pray together, and walk up the King's Highway. Lord, if You allow me to get this job, then I can come to service regularly because I can set my own hours."

We place the thing before the kingdom. Honey, that flesh is setting you up for failure. Please talk to the flesh and tell it to sit down somewhere!

That is opposite of the principle and God will not go contrary to what He has spoken. He is not like man that He will lie.

> **We place the thing before the kingdom.**

Ask…and it will be given.

Seek…and you will find.

Knock and it will be opened.

What exactly should we be asking, seeking, and knocking for?

> If you then, being evil, know how to give good gifts to your children, how much more will your Father who is in heaven give good things to those who ask Him! (Matthew 7:11, NKJV)

Hmmm, here is a thought! What are good gifts from an earthly parent and what are good gifts from a heavenly Father? Even what is considered *good* means something different to a child and an adult. From a child's perspective, a good gift may be the PS4, the latest smartphone, or virtual reality gadgets. From that parent's perspective, a trust fund or CD that the child cannot get until a certain age may be a good gift.

Just what is a good gift from a heavenly Father? He told us many times. One thing we can ask for is wisdom.

If any of you lacks wisdom, let him ask of God, who gives to all liberally and without reproach, and it will be given to him. (James 1:5, NKJV)

Here are some others found in 1 Corinthians 12:7-11:
- Word of knowledge
- Faith
- Gifts of healing
- Working of miracles
- Prophecy
- Discerning of spirits
- Diversities of tongues

The best gift of all is love.

And though I have the gift of prophecy, and understand all mysteries and all knowledge, and though I have all faith, so that I could remove mountains, but have not love, I am nothing. (1 Corinthians 13:2, NKJV)

Oh, so it makes sense now: If I keep asking, seeking, and knocking for love, faith, wisdom, or any of the spiritual gifts my heavenly Father gives, He will give it, I will find it, and the door will be opened. What door? The door to the kingdom of heaven.

And I will give you the keys of the kingdom of heaven, and whatever you bind on earth will be bound in heaven and whatever you loose on earth will be loosed in heaven. (Matthew 16:18, NKJV)

I can guarantee that you can look back over your life and there will be some proof that God has been there for you all the time. The question is where were you when He needed you? Had you been in position to answer to the call, as opposed to running from it, maybe the situation would have had different results.

The Lord desires to take that dry, ashy place in your life and turn it into a beautiful flower bed of blooming roses. He cannot do that if you will not remove yourself from the will of the flesh. Rise up out of your seat, and take hold of the duty and obligation that you were chosen to do.

Uh-oh, I had another thought. Sometimes I have imaginary conversations, but they are so real and transparent. Imagine this. After all the ranting and reminding the Lord of what He said in the Scripture about asking, seeking, and knocking, imagine Him responding:

"You asked Me, and yes, I did tell you to do that. I know what I said."

Ask, and it will be given to you; seek, and you will find; knock, and it will be opened to you. For everyone who asks receives, and he who seeks finds, and to him who knocks it will be opened. (Matthew 7:7-8 NKJV)

Thank you for the reminder, but I have asked some things of you as well. Do you remember?

"I asked you to repent and change your ways so they know how to.

"I asked you to forgive those who hurt you so they know how to.

"I asked you to live peacefully with all so they know how to.

"I asked you to humble yourself and pray and turn from evil so they know how to.

"I asked you to pray without stopping, so that they know how to.

"I asked you to be thankful and grateful in every situation, so that they know how to.

"I asked you to love them and you question their existence.

"I asked you to show them how to live righteously and you tell them without demonstration.

"I asked you to train and impart in them and you left them so you "could do you."

"I asked you to be patient, and you are giving up on them.

"I asked you to introduce them to Me but you can't because you do not know Me (you won't make time to spend with Me). I understand that you did not have the example you felt you deserved while growing up to do what I have asked you, but you really did have the example. I gave you the example of what not to do. Yet and still, that should not prevent you.

I'll show you, if you just listen. Then you'll experience My peace, which surpasses any human understanding."

> *...and the peace of God, which surpasses all understanding, will guard your hearts and minds through Christ Jesus.* (Philippians 4:7, NKJV)

"I gave you a gift and you viewed it as a curse."

> *Children are a gift from the LORD; they are a reward from him.* (Psalms 127:3, NLT)

"You have some things to ask of me and I am asking something of you: Who is teaching your children to know Me as their Lord and Savior?"

In case you're wondering, the story of Lazarus ends such that Jesus told the people that the sickness of Lazarus would reveal the glory of God. And so, Jesus raises him from the dead. I don't know about you, but I want Jesus to love me so, that He feels my tears and it moves Him to bring me from a situation that the enemy believed would place me on death row.

Flesh Assessment:
1. What are you doing right now that has you on death row?
2. What are you doing that is destroying your spiritual relationship with God, our Father? Confess it, call it out by name, and disconnect from anything associated with it. The jury found you guilty, but Jesus has acquitted you through grace and mercy.

It's time to tell the flesh bye! Bye Felicia!

Pause and Reflect

"What you want to accomplish in life and where
you are in the journey will determine what areas
you most need to think about today."

—JOHN C. MAXWELL

L et's take break for a moment, because we have been going in full throttle. Let's try a different angle to grasp this flesh thing.

Think of the person you love the most. Have you ever done something that just crushed him or her and the person's reaction to what you said or did hurt you to the core? Notice I said that it hurt *you*. How the person responded was not something you were prepared for. Maybe he was slow to respond. Maybe she may have not even uttered a word, but it was the expression on her face that causes you to drop your head in disgust. We have all been there. Hmmm, can you imagine disappointing our heavenly Father with nonsense? To the point, where He hangs His head in disgust, not having anything to say, at a loss for words?

Anytime we give in to sin, we frustrate the grace of God. From this point on, resolve not to do anything that will disappoint your Father. The best way to do that is separate from fleshly desires.

Pause and reflect on the mistakes you have made. Forgive yourself for them and disassociate from anything that would cause you to repeat the same process. Reflect on the accomplishments and victories you have won and build upon those to help you move forward. Learn how to keep yourself in the love of God.

But you, beloved, building yourselves up on your most holy faith and pray-
ing in the Holy Spirit, keep yourselves in the love of God, looking for the
mercy of our Lord Jesus Christ unto eternal life. (Jude 1:20-21, NKJV)

Life is about pause, reflect, and pursuit. You must resolve not to allow anyone or anything, including yourself, to stop you from celebrating the living hope that you have been given, even when your heart's desire is yet to be realized. God is greater than our hearts because He created them. Since He created them, He knows what would pull our hearts away from Him. We must therefore trust His plans for our lives.

Hope lives. God granted a hope that never dies, but this hope only manifests itself when we allow it to live through us. When we give up our own lives as a sacrifice to carry out the purpose of God, we are given a living hope in exchange. Just in case you are uncertain of that hope, it is Jesus.

Hope lives because Jesus is hope. His presence is felt everywhere, even during a worldwide catastrophic failure, Christ gave and continues to give us hope. I don't know about you, but I have something in view. I see my hope and I remember the promises of God through Jesus Christ. I know He lives, because He lives in me.

Blessed be the God and Father of our Lord Jesus Christ, who according to His abundant mercy has begotten us again to a living hope through the resurrection of Jesus Christ from the dead, 4 to an inheritance incorruptible and undefiled and that does not fade away, reserved in heaven for you. (1 Peter 1:3-4, NKJV)

Judgment vs. Discernment

"Judge not and lest ye be judged; twist not the
Scripture, lest ye be like Satan."

—PAUL WASHER

Okay, the break is over. Let's dive back in. God loves us so much that He saw we needed help. He sent us help. He sent us Jesus.

For God so loved the world, that he gave his only begotten Son, that whosoever believeth in him should not perish, but have everlasting life. (John 3:16, NKJV)

As believers and representatives of Jesus Christ, we are not supposed to judge others. If Jesus did not come to condemn, then who are we to work beyond His threshold of workmanship?

For God did not send His Son into the world to condemn the world, but that the world through Him might be saved. (John 3:17, NKJV)

The Bible clearly explains to us that Jesus was not sent here to condemn, criticize, or to make us suffer. He came to save us. What is amazing is how quickly we use a verse about not judging one another to justify our behavior. Many people use this Scripture:

Do not judge others, and you will not be judged. For you will be treated as you treat others. The standard you use in judging is the standard by which you will be judged. (Matthew7:1-2, NLT)

We take this verse to mean: "You don't have the right to tell me I'm wrong."

Can I share something with you? The Bible commands us that we do not judge others, but this does not mean we cannot and should not show discernment. If we are made in the image of God and we have His characteristics, described as the *fruit of the Spirit*, then we have the ability to identify sin.

Do not judge according to appearance, but judge with righteous judgment. (John 7:24, NKJV)

The intent of the Bible is not to figure out how we can do what we want. God did not send us His word for us to scramble through the pages and find a verse that supports our character, which represents the flesh and is the opposite of who He says we should be. Here is why we do not and should not judge or condemn:

The attitude and behavior of a person brings upon his or her own condemnation.

He who believes in Him is not condemned; but he who does not believe is condemned already, because he has not believed in the name of the only begotten Son of God. And this is the condemnation, that the light has come into the world, and men loved darkness rather than light, because their deeds were evil. For everyone practicing evil hates the light and does not come to the light, lest his deeds should be exposed. But he who does the truth comes to the light, that his deeds may be clearly seen, that they have been done in God. (John 3:18-21, NKJV)

Followers of Jesus are often accused of "judging" when they speak out against sin. But opposing sin is not wrong. Holding the standard of righteousness naturally opposes unrighteousness and brings up the defensive boxing gloves of those who choose sin over godliness.

We are not called to judge. Let us therefore not judge according to appearance but discern in the Spirit.

> **Holding the standard of righteousness naturally opposes unrighteousness and brings up the defensive boxing gloves of those who choose sin over godliness.**

OPPOSES - RESIST.

The Flesh vs. Your Flesh

"God will never tell us to do something that
gratifies the flesh."

—CHARLES STANLEY

Whenever we see the word *flesh*, we believe the physical body is being referenced. It is a fact, that flesh can be used to describe our physique. If we are honest, it is that physical appearance that gets us in trouble. How many times has your flesh caused problems? The color, texture, and length of hair and how the style compliments and accents her eyes; the smoothness and color of her skin when she wore the perfect color to compliment her skin tone. How his clothing draped over his physique so perfectly Oooh-la-laaa!

We are all the same on the inside, but the package is presented differently and uniquely, in such a way that it touches your soul. C'mon now! You did not come out the womb spiritual. Last I checked, John the Baptist was the only one filled from the womb. Well, thank You, Lord, for keeping it real with us. He shared with us the situation with King David and Bathsheba, just in case we needed a real-life example and the folks around us didn't want to keep it real. David wanted Bathsheba so much, you know how it goes, he had her husband killed. Really David? Bathsheba touched David's soul (2 Samuel 11).

Your soul is who you are. Your emotions are tied to who you have become. Large corporations have learned how to capitalize on consumers through strategic marketing. As soon as you finish watching Ryan Seacrest and the others at Time Square screaming: "Happy New Year," here comes the weight-loss commercials: Weight Watchers, Jenny Craig, Experience Fitness discounts, Insanity, T25, Nutribullet, all of it.

If you have paid close attention to how the word *flesh* has been used in this book, you will notice a distinction between *the flesh* and *flesh*. During the introduction of the book, where I explained the meaning behind every word that has been used in the title, I intentionally kept this phrase connected: *with the flesh*.

There are many times when the Scripture uses the word *flesh* to refer to the physical body. However, when *the* is placed before the word *flesh*, we are dealing with something else. Let me show you. The Bible refers to our physical flesh in this verse:

All flesh is as grass, and all the glory of man as the flower of the grass. The grass withers, And its flower falls away. (1 Peter 1:24, NKJV)

In other words, as older women would say, "Keep living." That Coke-bottle shape will require a girdle and those abs will disappear. Keep living! After five children, I'm a living witness.

However, when the Bible uses the phrase *the flesh*, we are talking about something more distinct and powerful than just your appearance. What does *the flesh* mean? It refers to that part of us that is alienated from God, which is sin. It is rebellious, unruly, stubborn, and out control, if not brought under subjection. *The* flesh is that part of us that does not want to be told what to do. *The* flesh is that part of us that does not want to be held accountable for our behavior but would rather make justifications. *The* flesh refuses correction and does not want to have a thing to do with being obedient to God. *The* flesh believes that it can function without guidance from the Holy Spirit. *The* flesh often desires something simply on the premise that it isn't supposed to do or have it; just because someone says it cannot, it wants to prove that it can.

- The flesh will make your mind drift off so fast while listening to the sermon on Sunday, until you realize you told your neighbor something, but it wasn't what the pastor told you to say.
- The flesh is an enemy against God because it is the enemy.
- The flesh is not subject to the law of God.

Because the carnal mind is enmity against God; for it is not subject to the law of God, nor indeed can be. So then, those who are in the flesh cannot please God. (Romans 8:7-8, NKJV)

Not only does the flesh fight against the spirit, it literally wages an all-out war:

Beloved, I beg you as sojourners and pilgrims, abstain from fleshly lusts which war against the soul. (1 Peter 2:11, NKJV)

If you don't think that the flesh is strong, grab the Bible. Not an app on your phone but a hard copy and just try to read for five minutes. Watch how quickly your mind begins to drift and think on anything but God. Pay attention to the texts and phone calls that come in at that time. Huh! Don't call yourself going on a fast. Watch how *the flesh* goes to war with the spirit.

The flesh is in direct conflict with the spirit. "The spirit" in this case refers not to the Holy Spirit but to the human spirit. The human spirit is the part of us that is open to God and desires to get to know Him. It is the part of us that is attracted and drawn to the goodness of God and desires to have a connection with our Savior. The Holy Spirit connects with our human spirit to lead and guide us once we surrender to the will of God. Without the Holy Spirit, we would be consumed by *the flesh*; but we must force *the* flesh to *shut up* and *sit down*.

The flesh is sin.

I say then: Walk in the Spirit, and you shall not fulfill the lust of the flesh. For the flesh lusts against the Spirit, and the Spirit against the flesh; and these are contrary to one another, so that you do not do the things that you wish. (Galatians 5:16-17, NKJV)

The flesh will direct you away from the Spirit.

For those who live according to the flesh set their minds on the things of the flesh, but those who live according to the Spirit, the things of the Spirit. (Romans 8:5, NKJV)

It is important for you to really understand the flesh. If God felt we could overcome *the* flesh on our own, why would Jesus send us the Holy

ENMITY- ENEMY or ENEMIES, hostility

Spirit to help us? Come on, you gotta see this. Our flesh cannot fight a spiritual war.

> *For the weapons of our warfare are not carnal but mighty in God for pulling down strongholds, casting down arguments and every high thing that exalts itself against the knowledge of God, and bringing every thought into captivity to the obedience of Christ.* (2 Corinthians 10:4-5, NKJV)

The enemy exalts himself against God and His knowledge. If you sow to your flesh or do things to please your flesh, you reap *the* flesh.

> *For he who sows to his flesh will of the flesh reap corruption, but he who sows to the Spirit will of the Spirit reap everlasting life.* (Galatians 6:8, NKJV)

What corruption will you experience in your own physical body?

> *Now the works of the flesh are evident, which are: adultery, fornication, uncleanness, lewdness, idolatry, sorcery, hatred, contentions, jealousies, outbursts of wrath, selfish ambitions, dissensions, heresies, envy, murders, drunkenness, revelries, and the like; of which I tell you beforehand, just as I also told you in time past, that those who practice such things will not inherit the kingdom of God.* (Galatians 5:19-21, NKJV)

When something becomes corrupted or corroded, what can it be used for? Stop allowing your flesh to be used, because the real you—your spirit—is decaying. You are gradually being destroyed. We were already forewarned that the enemy's job is to steal, kill, and to destroy (John 10:10), so what he does shouldn't be a surprise.

Do you have that set of serving utensils or dishes that you only bring out for special occasions? I seldom hear much about people doing that nowadays. I see more of paper plates and utensils being used because the cleanup after a dinner party is real! At least in my household, with all the children, I need to get it done and get it done quickly.

Large family gatherings mean the best food, fun, laughter, and "the good dishes." The colorful pots that matched the kitchen placed on the stove. The matching pot holders and dry towels for the dishes hung across the handle of the stove. Oh shoot! Forget washing dishes. Go ahead and use the dishwasher this one time out of the year. What makes these utensils and plates better than those for everyday use? They may be a bit more expensive. They could have been handed down from previous generations. Whatever the reason, bringing out these dishes meant the event itself was special to you, and you wanted the invited guests to feel the love, time, and energy you've taken to prepare for their attendance.

Just like those "good" dishes, we have been set aside for special use. The Bible calls this a living sacrifice. You see, unlike our good dishes and utensils, the Lord did not search for the most extravagant, eye-catching tool. We were the ugly Christmas sweater sent to Goodwill, deemed to be useless and cheap. We were the penny on the ground overlooked, stepped over, or stepped on, viewed as being worthless and not worth enough value to be picked up, cleaned off, and used.

When the Lord found you at your lowest place in life, it was not by mishap. It was on purpose. He does not think or behave like us. You know we want to be with the people who look like they have it together. Having blinded eyes, we look at people through our physical eyes and not with our hearts. We follow after the "in-crowd" as opposed to drawing the crowd to us through love and kindness as Jesus does. Just as soon as the person hits a low, runs out of money, or goes through some type of suffering that changes their routine, some turn their backs, just as Job's friends did to him. They murmured amongst themselves and said that Job *had* to have sinned against the Lord to have all of those bad things happen to him. Like most of us, when we see someone going through hard times, we assume they did something wrong.

God isn't like us. He sees what's on the inside of you. He knows what He has placed within you. God found Job worthy enough to withstand the attacks of the enemy because He knew Job's heart. God knew what He had instilled in Job and what Job allowed God to perfect through obedience to the word of God.

That same penny that's stepped over and looked down on, not worth your effort of bending over and picking up, is the only coin that can give *exact* change when the price difference between the item purchased and the money given to pay for it is uneven (you better catch this right here)!

Flesh Assessment:
1. Have you set yourself aside and apart from sin to be used by our Father for a special purpose that He has chosen just for you?

But in a great house there are not only vessels of gold and silver, but also of wood and clay, some for honor and some for dishonor. Therefore, if anyone cleanses himself from the latter, he will be a vessel for honor, sanctified and useful for the Master, prepared for every good work.
(2 Timothy 2:20-21, NKJV)

NOTES CHAPTER 7

LOVE

HOLY

HUMILITY

MERCY

KINDNESS

PATIENCE

SACRIFICE

ETERNAL

MEEKNESS

THE SPIRIT

GRACE

PEACE

COMPASSION

JOY

TEMPERENCE

CONSIDERATE

GENTLENESS

LIFE

INTEGRITY

Shut Up!

"Never miss a good chance to shut up."

—WILL ROGERS

The Spirit Response to the Flesh

D o you have siblings? If not, maybe you have cousins you grew up with that were like brothers or sisters. Have you ever encountered a situation where you were at odds with a family member? Maybe you didn't see eye-to-eye on something and you were not on good terms for a moment but it didn't matter because you're still family. You eventually got over it, but during that time, of separation, you caught wind that bae baeee somebody was bad-mouthing your relative. At that point, it didn't matter if you and that family member had a disagreement. Nobody else can talk crazy about your relative or there is going to be a situation.

Here I go: I had another imaginative thought about me having this conversation about my family with someone who was talking crazy. I wanted to share it with you, but first think about this: when we are in a relationship with God, we should have that same level of loyalty and commitment that we would have to that person we will defend at all cost. See, God, is my Father and Jesus is my big brother…this is MY family now!

We have been adopted into a royal priesthood:

But you are a chosen generation, a royal priesthood, a holy nation,
His own special people, that you may proclaim the praises of Him who
called you out of darkness into His marvelous light; who once were not
a people but are now the people of God, who had not obtained mercy
but now have obtained mercy. (1 Peter 2:9-10, NKJV)

My imaginary conversation...

So now, that I am in the family, I have a relationship. God is my Father. Jesus is my brother. I will not accept you speaking ill against my family. It's kinda like this. I can't snap off because that's not how my Father raised me. He told me to act like I had some home training. Now that I'm a part of the royal family now, I must behave like it. I have been spiritually raised, I must walk with integrity. My Father taught me how to have some dignity and respect about myself so that I find favor with enemies and friends, and if I respond in any other way, I will disappoint Him and I simply cannot do that.

Train up a child in the way he should go, and when he is old he will not depart from it. (Proverbs 22:6, NKJV)

So...now, I hear you talking and saying my Father is not real, and all this here crap about the universe, and scientifically proven facts and all this gurgling. I do not know why I let this get to me, because you are speaking what you do not understand. You really have these emotions because my Father did not do what you had asked Him to and to be real, He should not have. Don't get it twisted. My Father is not crazy. He knows when someone is trying to take advantage of Him, so puh-lease... don't try to use my Father. That is not right! The reality is, He did not do "it" because you approached Him as if He owes you. Someone must have introduced you to my Father as a loan officer and not as a caregiver. Maybe you were introduced by one of His play children!

Remember back in the day, we would say, "That's my play cousin"? Whelp, you met somebody that was pretending to be an heir to the thrown of grace. They pretended to know who God the Father is. They pretended to be related to Jesus, but they had no features. They had no characteristics. There are no traits. When you're adopted into the family, you look like my Father. You act like Him. Your mannerisms are like Him.

But the fruit of the Spirit is love, joy, peace, longsuffering, kindness, goodness, faithfulness, gentleness, self-control. Against such there is no law. (Galatians 5:22-23, NKJV)

If I sit here and listen to you belittling my Father and my Brother, now I'm crazy. Because I know the type of beings They are and how They have

Whelp - to give birth to the young: Said of some animals.

only desired to help people. Since you talking crazy, I know who and what I'm dealing with and I'll just fall back. I'll study (learn to be quiet, as my Father instructed me).

But avoid foolish and ignorant disputes, knowing that they generate strife. And a servant of the Lord must not quarrel but be gentle to all, able to teach, patient, in humility correcting those who are in opposition, if God perhaps will grant them repentance, so that they may know the truth, and that they may come to their senses and escape the snare of the devil, having been taken captive by him to do his will. (2 Timothy 2:23-26, NKJV)

I pray that my Father continues to have mercy on you. Once you've come to your senses, you'll be looking to speak with me again. When that moment arrives, you'll be ready to proceed with the adoption hearing.

...having predestined us to adoption as sons by Jesus Christ to Himself, according to the good pleasure of His will. (Ephesians 1:5, NKJV)

But until then...be careful how you talk to and about my Father—He plays no games!

Do not be rash with your mouth, and let not your heart utter anything hastily before God. For God is in heaven, and you on earth; Therefore, let your words be few. (Ecclesiastes 5:2, NKJV)

That was a reenactment I had in my head of me speaking to someone who questions the power of God and the authenticity of Jesus Christ. When will we have that kind of loyalty and commitment toward Them, that no matter what, we are committed, dedicated, and passionate about our Savior, who He is, and what He means to us?

Who He Is

"Excuse me, do I know you?"

—Evan Almighty

The Proper Introduction

If I always introduce God as
- A supplier of needs
- A prayer answerer
- A need supplier

Then I am setting you up to only speak with Him when you need something. For example, if my children introduce me to their friends as the person from whom they can get whatever they want, and not their mother, imagine how that would make me feel? I would stand in the midst of them feeling crushed, heartbroken, used, and irrelevant. I would feel as if my parental relationship means nothing to them. By hearing this sort of introduction, their friends are set up to approach me with the thought of only getting what they want, not for the value I have added to the lives of my babies or who we represent as a family.

Imagine how God, our Father, feels.

✦ It is critical for us as followers of Jesus to introduce God as our Father. A father loves. A father corrects. A father teaches his children how to become adults and how to handle tough situations. A father teaches his children how to have respect for themselves and others. A father nurtures and protects.

In the book of Acts, there is a story about a man by the name of Philip. The Spirit of the Lord told him to get up and go in a certain direction. As he was going he came across a man of high authority. The Bible says he held a high-ranking position for Queen Candace. Philip heard the man of authority reading the book of Isaiah. The Spirit spoke to Philip and told him to converse with the man. Philip asked the man if he understood what he was reading. In a nutshell, he replied by saying it is impossible for him to understand if he did not have someone to teach him.

If we do not teach people to repent, if we do not teach people to separate from sin, if we do not teach people to be respectful in God's house, if we do not teach about JESUS, how will the people experience peace? How will they learn to whom they can turn to in tumultuous times?

How can they become passionate about someone who hasn't been properly introduced?

＊Jesus has standards and what is so wrong with that? If someone approaches you to make an advance or get your number, within ten secs, while the person is walking up, you have sized him or her up physically. If this person doesn't fit your general preferences, you are immediately turned off.

＊If God says separate from sin and then He will receive you, why is that wrong? If Jesus says, God does not hear sinner's prayer, why is that wrong? Do you really know why He says this? I may sound like a broken record, but it doesn't seem apparent that the devil is the enemy of God; otherwise we would not do things in support of him.

＊ The devil is the enemy of God. He has openly professed to exalt his kingdom above God's. He's basically saying, "I can do what You do but better. Why are You God? I can be a god, too."

＊ Everything and anything that looks like His enemy, God will have no part. Imagine you having an enemy and your child, your sister, or your brother knows this person does not like you and does every undermining thing to hurt you; yet your family member still decides to retain this person as a dear friend. How would *you* feel?

＊ Sin is an adjective of the enemy and when you decide to associate with either of them, that separates you from the Lord.

> *Behold, the Lord's hand is not shortened, that it cannot save; Nor His ear heavy, That it cannot hear. But your iniquities have separated you from your God; and your sins have hidden His face from you, so that He will not hear. (Isaiah 59:1-2, NKJV)*

✦ Basically, you are telling God, your Father, "Aw Dad, the devil, he cool people. The devil is my friend." So, God in turn says, "Wow! Okay, well, you have just decided to become my enemy as well."

✦ *Adulterers and adulteresses! Do you not know that friendship with the world is enmity with God? Whoever therefore wants to be a friend of the world makes himself an enemy of God. Therefore, submit to God. Resist the devil and he will flee from you. Draw near to God and He will draw near to you. Cleanse your hands, you sinners; and purify your hearts, you double-minded.* (James 4:4, 7-8, NKJV)

It's time to start introducing the children of God to their heavenly Father so that they can have a real relationship with Him.

✦ I have read and heard many stories of people who grew up in foster homes or who were adopted and when they became of age, they wanted to meet their birth parents. Once the formal introduction is done, a decision to pursue a relationship has to be made; rebuilding and trust has to occur. More meetings, more discussions of why and what happened are necessary. A bond is being created; a relationship is being birthed.

One thing have I desired of the LORD, that will I seek after; that I may dwell in the house of the LORD all the days of my life, to behold the beauty of the LORD, and to inquire in his temple. (Psalms 27:4, NKJV)

What one thing have you desired of the Lord? Have you sought a relationship with Him, not based on what He can provide for you?

Are we birthing spiritual relationships? Are we birthing a desire for others to share in our joy and to know our Father or are we birthing spiritual abusers and users?

Who I Am

"Hi! My Name Is…"

—Eminem

Did I catch you off guard, using a line from a rapper? That is what we need to do to our spirit. Get up! Wake up your spirit to life. It is time for us to be intentional. To do this, we must know who we are. Therefore, I would like to provide you with a formal introduction of who I am, but before I do that, I must first tell you where I came from and about my background (aw shucks I'm excited).

My Father is God. Yep, the Creator, and I say that with so much pride and humility. For me to be the daughter of God, the Master Designer? I am daily in awe. My Brother's name is Jesus. He is my Savior. He rescued me when I did not want to be bothered. He is always looking out for me. I just love Him because He loved me, even when I rejected Him and told Him to leave me alone. I wouldn't dare tell Him that to His face, but my attitude sure did express it. He truly looks out for me. I could not have asked for a better big brother. Let me give a better introduction of who they are. That will enable you to better understand who I am.

God revealed Himself to us and He makes that certain we understand that everything originates from Him, through Him, and was made by Him. First, God introduced Himself to us:

And God said to Moses, "I AM WHO I AM." And He said, "Thus you shall say to the children of Israel, 'I AM has sent me to you.'" (Exodus 3:14 NKJV)

God is "I AM." What does this mean? He is whatever we need Him to be. The Holy Spirit strategically used "am" which is present tense, to describe God. The Bible says: "I Am," not "I was." God is not dead. He is real,

He is alive, and He is well. He is "I Am!" (Oh glory, I just inserted a praise break. Okay, okay, let me stay on point.)

We then learned that God took a portion of Himself and made Himself as flesh to go through everything we experience here on this earth. He created Himself a son and gave Him a name above all names. I have five children, lost one, so a total of six. Every time my husband and I would research names, I would look up the meaning of the names. God named His son Jesus and gave us the meaning:

> *"Behold, the virgin shall be with child, and bear a Son, and they shall call His name Immanuel," which is translated, "God with us."* (Matthew 1:23, NKJV)

God gave us a physical image of who He is, through His son, Jesus.

> *He is the image of the invisible God, the firstborn over all creation. For by Him all things were created that are in heaven and that are on earth, visible and invisible, whether thrones or dominions or principalities or powers. All things were created through Him and for Him.* (Colossians 1:15-16 , NKJV)

Jesus then tells us who He is (not was):
I am the way!

> *Jesus replied, "I am the way, and the truth, and the life. No one comes to the Father except through me.* (John 14:6, NKJV)

I am the bread of life!

> *Jesus said to them, "I am the bread of life. The one who comes to me will never go hungry, and the one who believes in me will never be thirsty.* (John 6:35, NKJV)

I am the good shepherd.

> *"I am the good shepherd. The good shepherd lays down his life for the sheep."* (John 10:11, NKJV).

I am the door.

"I am the door. If anyone enters through me, he will be saved, and will come in and go out, and find pasture." (John 10:9, NKJV)

I am the light of the world.

Then Jesus spoke out again, "I am the light of the world. The one who follows me will never walk in darkness, but will have the light of life." (John 8:12, NKJV)

I am the resurrection and life.

Jesus said to her, "I am the resurrection and the life. The one who believes in me will live even if he dies..." (John 11:25, NKJV)

I am the vine.

"I am the vine; you are the branches. The one who remains in me – and I in him – bears much fruit, because apart from me you can accomplish nothing." (John 15:5, NKJV)

Through the Scriptures, Jesus reaffirms that He and God are one.

"I and My Father are one." (John 10:30, NKJV)

Then the Jews said to Him, "You are not yet fifty years old, and have You seen Abraham?" Jesus said to them, "Most assuredly, I say to you, before Abraham was, I AM." (John 8:57-58, NKJV)

If you look at who God introduces Himself as and who Jesus introduces Himself as in the examples I just shared, replace the "I Am" statements with "God."
God the way.
God the vine.
God the good shepherd.
God the light of the world.

God the door.
God the bread of life.
God the resurrection.
Oh my God this is so powerful to me! They are ONE! "I AM" is God. Jesus is God in the flesh. Once we know who God, our Father, is, and who Jesus, our Savior, is, They affirm who They are in us, by the Spirit of God (The Holy Spirit).

Jesus answered and said unto him, "If a man love me, he will keep my words: and my Father will love him, and we will come unto him, and make our abode with him." (John 14:23, KJV)

Here is when it gets real! Lord, I thank You! Now you have been affirmed by the Spirit of the living God. You know who you are, whose you are, and what you have on the inside of you. You can introduce yourself to this lost world, as a representative of Jesus Christ, for the glory of God.

Now, that I have given you a little background of my family tree, please allow me to provide you with a proper introduction of who I am…

I am the salt of the earth. (Matthew 5:13)
I am the light of the world. (Matthew 5:14)
I am a child of God. (John 1:12)
I am a royal priesthood. (1 Peter 2:9-10)
I am a branch. (John 15:5)
I am the temple of the living God. (Romans 12:1)
I am more than a conqueror. (Romans 8:37)
I am anointed by God. (1 John 2:27)
I am a new creature. (2 Corinthians 5:17)
I am a peacemaker. (Matthew 5:9)
I am healed. (Isaiah 53:5)
I am saved. (2 Timothy 1:9)
I am a victor not a victim. (1 Corinthians 15:57)
I am…and you are…because He is!

Who You Are

"Prized Possession: Something you care deeply
for, above all else."

—ALAN SMYTH

When I was a child, I loved playing with Barbie dolls. I enjoyed dressing them and attempting to comb their hair the way I saw my mom combing mine. I tried braiding, twisting, and even using hair balls. I remember one Christmas, my mom purchased a doll that was taller than the traditional Barbie doll. When the doll moved, it appeared that her eyelids would close, as if she were blinking. That was UH-mazing!

My dolls were special to me. Although I did not create them myself, they were mine because they were purchased for me. I could dress them the way that I desired, and I did not want to share them with anyone. I needed my baby dolls. Growing up as an only child, they kept me company in my "play" world at home.

Do you know that we are more precious to God than my baby dolls were to me? Sure, God made angels, but He wanted something specifically designed the way He desired. He wanted someone that looked like Him, someone He could see Himself through.

So God created man in His own image; in the image of God He created him; male and female He created them. (Genesis 1:27, NKJV)

Have you ever watched your children and identified the mannerisms they have that are similar to yours? Then you smiled in amazement and wonder for the gift God has given you. That is what God, our Father, desired. He wanted someone that He could give some of His knowledge, to think like Him.

For the Lord gives wisdom; from His mouth come knowledge and understanding. (Proverbs 2:6, NKJV)

He wanted something He could breathe His breath into; and thus we were born, fearfully and wonderfully, we were created. We were made to be like our Father; we are His children. Some of us He created with blonde hair and blue eyes. Some He created with brown hair and brown eyes. Some short and some tall in stature; but we were designed just as He desired.

Everyone who is called by My name, Whom I have created for My glory; I have formed him, yes, I have made him. (Isaiah 43:7, NKJV)

Just as my tall doll could open and close her eyes, an ability that was quite the opposite of the popular Barbie dolls, God decided His children would have special gifts as well. Some have an uncanny ability to sing. Others are great with managing business. Some have athletic abilities like no other. And there are some who have multiple gifts. Then our loving Father placed purpose in our lives that align with the gifts He has given us. Just as I dressed up my dolls the way I desired, everything we were given, how we were created and why, are all done to please our Father.

Here is what puzzles me: when we realize what is purposed in us, and our Father says He really needs us to operate in our purpose, we say: "I'm not ready yet!"

So, basically, we're saying we are not ready to do something that was designed for us to do? That is like my doll telling me, "I don't like my hair." First, the doll would be burned and tossed in a dumpster far away from my home —uh uh. The Chucky doll would not become a reality in my life. But if talking back is a characteristic of the doll, my reaction would be one of: "Who are you? You do realize I can replace you, right?"

Can you imagine our Father thinking: "I gave you a gift and a purpose and the benefits are for you, but because you are not ready, I should wait on you?"

You know, it baffles me that we talk to God like we have all power and control over our own lives. While we continue to resist, we have the audacity to have a "by the way spirit…"

✘ No, I'm not ready, but by the way…can You continue to grant me grace and mercy, until I am ready?

Can You continue to keep me?

Can You continue to give me good health to do what I want to do?

Can You bless me with a spouse?

I need this higher paying job; can You open a door?

We intentionally wander through life because we told our Father, "I'm not ready." If not careful, we soon become lost.

Just as I became upset and frustrated if I lost my dolls, our Father became upset when we were lost. In fact, the Bible, from the beginning until the end, proves that God has done everything to find us and for us—His prized possession—to find Him. Even Jesus was sent…for us. He sent someone to die just for us, to bring us back to Him!

Here is how we became lost. God created this angel named Lucifer. As far as beauty, there was none like him. He was arrayed in jewels and stones, some of which I have never heard of or seen in today's time. Lucifer was also a musician. One day, he got beside himself (Ezekiel 28:13-17). He became prideful and conceited. Isaiah 14:12-14 explains how the enemy decided to make his own kingdom and attempt to make it greater than God's. Let me ask you this: when you find out someone is trying to set you up and take what is yours, what would you do? You would have nothing more to do with the person. That's what God, our Father, did. He got rid of His enemy.

The enemy, Lucifer, and some of the angels that sided with him, lost their place in heaven. When God created us, Satan presented himself with Adam and Eve, so that we could lose out as well. The enemy wants to destroy us because he can't get back to that heavenly place. So, the war that has been made is between God and the devil.

We, as God's most precious creation that He designed especially for Himself, happen to be caught in the middle. The enemy attacks God's most prized possession—you. Yes, you, the one who continues to say: "I'm not ready yet."

Here is what we miss: the enemy has been in heaven. He has been in the presence of our Father. He has even walked in the Garden of Eden.

You were in Eden, the garden of God; Every precious stone was your covering: The sardius, topaz, and diamond, Beryl, onyx, and jasper, Sapphire, turquoise, and emerald with gold. The workmanship of your timbrels and pipes Was prepared for you on the day you were created. We have not! (Ezekiel 28:13, NKJV)

Here is what we miss: the enemy has been in heaven. He has been in the presence of our Father. He has even walked in the Garden of Eden.

Think about that. The very one who seeks to steal, kill, and destroy you has been where your Father lives. Huntay, that place has to be special for the enemy to go through great lengths at preventing us from being in the presence of our Father. Don't you see this? If you had been in the presence of God, you pretty much know how God is, you know what He can do, and you know what you are up against, right? Satan knows this! He knows that he is no match for the Almighty, but he also recognizes and is smart enough to realize that we have not valued the relationship that our Father is trying to have with us, through Jesus. The enemy knows that once we get so close to our Father and truly surrender, there is nothing he can do against an all-powerful and all-knowing God. So, the enemy plays tricks on us.

I've seen movies where if a person could not get to the one they were trying to hurt, they would hurt their family or the very thing they love the most, their prized possession. Remember the movie *Taken*? What about the action movie starring Jamie Foxx titled *Sleepless?* That is what the enemy does and continues to do. He is trying to upset God by destroying us and he is doing a great job, simply because "we are not ready yet."

We fight one another. We kill one another. We abuse our women and molest our children. Our children disrespect adults. The enemy makes us feel depressed and suicidal. We gossip, debate, argue, and hate one another. We find excuses to do what we want and indulge in the lust of the world and we make it convenient for us. We become prideful. All for what? We fall right into the schemes of the devil. No doubt, the enemy probably calls us stupid because here we have a piece of God, His Spirit, called the Holy Spirit, to live in us and guide us and we deliberately ignore Him because "We are not ready yet." We are the prized possession of God!

T W E L V E

Guilty as Charged

Involuntary Manslaughter

You have found yourself in a place that is not you. Something has happened. Routine has become the norm. There was a time when people would smile from your smile. People would come to you for advice or just to be in your presence because of your character and compassion.

Life. The choices that you made, and the enemy himself have all but made you into a parked car. You're stiff. You're not moving. Nothing is coming in and nothing is going out. You feel stuck. You're rash and abrasive with your words. You're angry. You're…just…here!

You have been charged with "involuntary manslaughter"!

Involuntary means "not done consciously." Manslaughter means "the failure to perform a legal duty expressly required to safeguard human life."

You have stopped performing your spiritual legal duty. The reality is that you didn't even recognize how you had changed. It just sorta…well… happened. Life. Just. Happened. You became busy. Busy at not doing the work of the Lord, which happens to be another ploy of the enemy.

I have some exciting news for you. The Supreme Court Judge, The King of Kings and Lord of Lords, Jesus has summoned you. You have been charged and ordered to do community service. Yep. Community service. You see, ALLLLL the anointing you have is not for one stationary location.

is time to come up from your seated position. You have told the flesh to shut up and sit down. Now, your seated position is uncomfortable. You are at the edge of the seat, bracing yourself to take a stand and it is now becoming clearer.

It's no wonder they don't like you on your job. It makes sense now as to why your children are being disrespectful in your home. It makes sense why the enemy is attacking your mind.

The anointing on your life can shift the atmosphere. If the enemy can get you to dwell on the issue that you're facing—yep, that issue that is staring you right back in the face—then he can immobilize your anointing and keep you operating in the flesh.

What you don't realize is when you deny yourself for the glory of God, God must move on your situation. What you have quickly forgotten is that there is power in what we speak. Speak to the issue about the power that your Father has.

On today, I will speak through the pages of this book, over your life. Your job is to believe!

You were ordained to go into the dark places. You were chosen to reach the unruly. You were handpicked to educate the most disruptive and rude children in the classrooms. You were called upon to bring to life those whose vision has become distorted and dormant. You were selected to lose that family member that meant so much to you. You were favored to have a failed marriage. You were elected to be ostracized by your family.

Your pain has produced possibility.

Let's sit this on the table though. The possibilities aren't clear when the pain is present. When my husband and I lost, what would have been our fourth child, you could not tell me that there was something positive on the other side of that pain.

I was in the Lord, married, and doing everything I knew to represent Jesus well. We were foretold that we would have a son. At that time, we already had three girls. When I found out that I was pregnant, I immediately thought, *this could be our son.* However, I never found out the sex of the child. On Wednesday, November 26, 2008, the day before Thanksgiving, I miscarried at two and a half months.

Questions filled my mind. I was angry and frustrated. I wanted to know if I had angered my Father or if I had done something to offend my

Savior. I thought of women who lived life without conscience and seemed to have no issues with pregnancy. They just pop them out like popping ice cubes from an ice tray.

I wanted to ask God why, but not come off rude. Honey, listen. I realize God can destroy an entire country in one day and make it completely disappear with no trace of existence except through word of mouth. Umm, I'm not stupid to approach Him as if He owes me anything. Two more children later, I realized what the possibilities were and are. Your problems produce pain. Your pain produces a war cry. Your war cry produces a war story.

It is possible that the child could have had a birth defect that would have been too much to bear with our large family. So, my Father implemented a little pain management on my behalf. It's possible that I would have experienced health complications during delivery and my Father blocked it. It's possible for me to now minister my pain to help others get through their pain and achieve their purpose.

> **Your problems produce pain. Your pain produces a war cry. Your war cry produces a war story.**

I have had to share with women my agony and frustrations with this particular pain on countless times. I came to the realization that as long as I humble myself as a servant of Jesus Christ, there is possibility in my pain, because Jesus is in the midst of my problems.

But Jesus looked at them and said, "with men it is impossible, but not with God; for with God all things are possible." (Mark 10:27, NKJV)

All your pain and frustration serves a greater purpose. Everything is coming together to develop you and wean you from the spiritual bottle and prepare you for adulthood. It's possible to push through the pain and to really grow and learn from it because Jesus is there. He is comforting you, promoting you, and cheering you on to get through it.

> **There's purpose on the other side of pain. Push through and deliver the purpose.**

There's purpose on the other side of pain. Push through and deliver the purpose.

There are those who cannot go it alone and they will need you to grab them and pull them out of their valley moment. Even in the darkest places, light brings a change. In the valley is where we see the hand of God. In the valley is where Jesus performs His miracles. When rain pours, and falls from the top of the mountain because the mountaintop can no longer hold all of the water, the valley is designed to catch the overflow. What am I saying? Even in the valley of life, you are still blessed. Even in the valley, the Lord is still with you.

Yea, though I walk through the valley of the shadow of death, I will fear no evil; for You are with me; Your rod and Your staff, they comfort me. (Psalm 23:4, NKJV)

Get up! Reconnect with power source and rekindle your flame. There are people waiting to hear from you. Their situation cannot change and neither will yours because you have been sitting in a parked car.

I, therefore, the prisoner of the Lord, beseech you to walk worthy of the calling with which you were called, with all lowliness and gentleness, with longsuffering, bearing with one another in love, endeavoring to keep the unity of the Spirit in the bond of peace. There is one body and one Spirit, just as you were called in one hope of your calling; from whom the whole body, joined and knit together by what every joint supplies, according to the effective working by which every part does its share, causes growth of the body for the edifying of itself in love. if indeed you have heard Him and have been taught by Him, as the truth is in Jesus: that you put off, concerning your former conduct, the old man which grows corrupt according to the deceitful lusts, and be renewed in the spirit of your mind. (Ephesians 4:1-4, 16, NKJV)

Breathe Again

"Breathe again, breathe again."

—TONI BRAXTON

What if I told you the enemy was trying to take your breath away?

So He said to them, "When you pray, say: Our Father in heaven, Hallowed be Your name. Your kingdom come. Your will be done on earth as it is in heaven. (Luke 11:2, NKJV)

Prayer is your connection with the kingdom of heaven. Prayer is your contact with who we really are, spiritual beings in a carnal world. Prayer keeps us honest with ourselves and vulnerable enough to recognize we are dependent on the Spirit for help.

How would you feel if you were an afterthought? Most times, we pray as an afterthought: after we have been beat down with responsibilities from work and family, we freshen up, climb into bed, take a deep breath, and say, "Oh…let me pray."

Anything you feel is important, you will make time for. How often do we excuse ourselves and con our minds into believing that these two minutes before we drool on our pillow is all the time we can afford? Let me ask you a question: If your breath were dependent upon your prayer life with the Lord, would you be breathing right now? If your communication with

God was contingent upon how much you pray, how much air would you have to breathe? Would you be alive?

The breath that you breathe is the Spirit that God blew into your nostrils to create you. Therefore, we must use this breath to uplift Him, to speak to Him, about Him and Him through us.

Jesus was and is a "fresh breath." First, He was flesh and then He was breath.

Jesus became flesh.

And the Word became flesh and dwelt among us, and we beheld His glory, the glory as of the only begotten of the Father, full of grace and truth. (John 1:14, NKJV)

Jesus became breath.

And when He had said this, He breathed on them, and said to them, "Receive the Holy Spirit." (John 20:22, NKJV)

Ahhhh a breath of fresh air that is Jesus! The enemy is trying to take your breath away—your connection with Jesus, through prayer. Don't cut off your lifeline. Your life is suffocating and you cannot breathe because you have stiffened it through the lack of communication through your prayer life. Take time to establish a relationship through prayer so that you can breathe again.

NOTES CHAPTER 13

When the Hurt and Healer Collide

The Victory: When Super met natural

You gave your heart. It was not planned, it just happened. Why? Because you love to love, and you love the idea of being loved. You love seeing others happy. You love the way love feels. The only issue is that you understand what love is and how it feels. It has been given to you all of your life through parents and loved ones, but those you have recently connected with have yet to learn the real meaning of love. Through the years, your love has been displaced. Repeatedly, the same result, different characters. Now, you have learned to love like the others and their definition of love—with emotions, one-sided, receiving what you can, just as long as you are not hurt. You have become "them." You have become just like the ones who did not know how to love like you; the ones who were unable to take the broken pieces and reconnect them to become whole. This time, you are the one left with fragments scattered everywhere. The love you were birthed with has now become loathing, a very strong feeling of disgust and hatred. You hate how you care and you are disgusted that you were blindsided multiple times. Not just in marital relationships, but in friendships, sibling relationships, and business ventures, hurt seems to follow you. Love is no longer an action word. It is an untouchable, unreachable, unimaginable dream.

Life wasn't great, but it was tolerable. You had the ability to do what you desired. You were able to get up early and stay up late without any adverse effects on your health. Your job was not ideal, but hey, at least you had income to pay your bills and buy something every now and then. Then "it" happened. It seemed out of nowhere, from a routine checkup, the doctors found "something." You have been diagnosed with…but how? You ate clean and fairly healthy. You did a few random exercises here and there. You lived a clean life, for the most part at least.

The words of the family practitioner continue ringing in your ears: "You need this, you need that; this pill will combat this, but it has this side effect." *Oh, Jesus what did I do to deserve this?* you thought. You cannot work a full-time job because of this…this…ailment. You cannot sleep through the night and it is difficult during the day to…just. do. anything. What was once an afterthought, to just get up and go, now takes preparation. What will you do now? The suffering and the hurt.

Life told you to give up, but then you met the Healer. Life said there is no such thing as real love, but then you met…the Healer. Life said accept the cards that were dealt, this will be the death of you. Then. You. Met. THE. Healer.

> **Life told you to give up, but then you met the Healer. Life said there is no such thing as real love, but then you met… the Healer. Life said accept the cards that were dealt, this will be the death of you. Then. You. Met. THE. Healer.**

You were truly introduced to the Healer, and although while growing up, you connected with genuine love, as you became an adult, you were acquainted with lust. But now you found love again. You are in love again, and you do not care what people say. Spat in His face, brought to open shame, to pull you from your pain. He is acquainted with your grief because He has experienced it also. He knows what it feels like to be rejected and used, when all He ever wanted to do was love and demonstrate what it really means. The Healer.

He was despised and rejected— a man of sorrows, acquainted with deepest grief. We turned our backs on him and looked the other way. He was despised, and we did not care. (Isaiah 53:3, NLT)

...The Healer

The Healer showed you what unconditional love really is. You knew it existed—you were just seeking for it in the wrong places and with the wrong guidance.

Many times, He has touched situations that seemed irreparable. A woman who had blood issues for 12 years. A man who had everything and lost it all, a man who had a disease where his own kind rejected him and required him to call out "Unclean, unclean!" Jesus specializes in miracles but has one requirement: that our faith be rooted and grounded in Him. Because of sin, diseases of all sorts and every imaginable evil entered the world. So, He entered the world and took the punishment of death that you deserved and has proven to you that He can do the impossible...IF you believe. The Healer.

But He was wounded for our transgressions, He was bruised for our iniquities; the chastisement for our peace was upon Him, and by His stripes we are healed. (Isaiah 53:5, NKJV)

When glory meets my suffering.
When mercy meets majesty.
When the hurt meets the Healer, you are made alive.

Jesus said to him, "If you can believe, all things are possible to him who believes." (Mark 9:23, NKJV)

Jesus told us in this world we would have troubles (John 16:33), but dealing with any degree of suffering is challenging. If we are not careful, we slowly disconnect from the comforting arms of our Savior. We may not ever understand the reasons for our particular trials, but one thing is for certain, those of us who truly love God, our trials work for us, not against us.

And we know that all things work together for good to those who love God, to those who are the called according to His purpose. (Romans 8:28, NKJV)

I encourage you to trust Jesus. Fall into His arms. Through all your rejection, He found glory in and through you. Allow Him to break all your fears and doubt. The Healer is waiting to heal your hurt.

*Never! Can a mother forget her nursing child? Can she feel no love
for the child she has borne? But even if that were possible, I would not
forget you! See, I have written your name on the palms of my hands...*
(Isaiah 49:15-16, NLT)

When the hurt and the Healer collide, grace and mercy restores and
realigns us back under the will of our Father. When the hurt and the Healer
collide, get ready for a collision course with greatness. Your destiny awaits
you. Stand up and take your rightful place.

NOTES CHAPTER 14

FIFTEEN

I Wanna Be Where You Are

"For your glory, I will do anything. Just to see you, to behold you as my King. I wanna be where you are."

—TASHA COBBS

Being in the presence of God and experiencing the power of the Holy Spirit will make your spirit yearn to be with Him. There is no greater presence to be in. There is no better company to keep. If we can experience a portion of His power here on Earth, can you imagine what it would be like to live in His presence, where the angels worship and His throne resides?

Just as we long to be close to Him, God our Father, desires to be with us. God wants to be where we are. The book of Exodus explains how God delivered His children from the hand of Pharaoh by Moses. It then provides the laws or commandments on how God's children should conduct themselves.

Chapters 1-7 depicts how Israel was enslaved, the story of Moses, and how he arose to be Israel's leader and to send warning to Pharaoh about freeing God's children.

In chapters 7-13 God begins to release plagues to let Pharaoh know that He was speaking through Moses and He wasn't playing no games.

Chapters 14-18 tell of how Israel "exited" Egypt and was allowed to leave. Then Pharaoh changes his mind, decides to go after them, and we see how God parts the Red Sea for His babies but drowns their enemies.

In chapters 19-24, Israel is free from slavery and now they need to adhere to what God our Father commands. He was setting them up to inherit a blessing.

Chapter 25 is where it gets interesting. God says to His people: "I heard your cries for help. To be delivered from the yoke of bondage. I raised up a leader amongst you—in the presence of your enemy and made him your footstool. I showed you that Moses was real and a true man of God, who received commandment from me, by allowing everything he said would happen, to come to pass. I showed you that I am bigger than your biggest enemy—I AM sovereign. Then I allowed you to 'exit' the building with confidence and assurance that I love you and I have chosen you above all."

God says, "Now…I wanna be where you are."

In Exodus 25:8, God gave Moses a command to tell the children of Israel to make Him a temple. Why? Because He wanted to be among His children. Oh my Father! That is so powerful and loving. Glory to Your name, Jesus.

And let them make Me a sanctuary, that I may dwell among them. (Exodus 25:8, NKJV)

As preparations are made for God's temple, He is meticulous, thorough and methodical. He is specific and He is detailed. God says, "I will tell you exactly how I want my sanctuary to be built and you will build it how I tell you (all explained in the latter versus of Exodus 25). First the people are going sacrifice the best to make Me the best (orders given for a collection) You're going to give willingly and from your heart. You will use materials with specific colors of blue, purple, and scarlet, specific wood, and gold."

God speaks about the Ark of the Covenant and its details. The Ark is where the law was written, also called the testimony, because it is there where God testified of His will. The testimony served two purposes: written proof of what God said and a testimony against the children of Israel if they disobeyed. God always provides a witness and proof.

God proceeds to explain the dimensions of the mercy seat and the construction and direction of the cherubim that would spread over it. He even gave the position of spoons and dishes, the candlesticks and lampstands and their purpose.

Talk about being a project manager. Why? Why would God be so picky about His sanctuary? Why would He give so many details? The sanctuary being built would be a copy of His throne in heaven.

That is why, the tabernacle and everything in it, which were copies of things in heaven, had to be purified by the blood of animals. But the real things in heaven had to be purified with far better sacrifices than the blood of animals. (Hebrews 9:23, NLT)

God gave specific instructions on how to build His sanctuary. God gave specific instructions on how Noah would build the ark. Noah could not enter the ark if there was no righteousness in Him. That ark would become a sanctuary built unto God. What am I saying to you today? If God was specific and detailed about a building, made by the hands of men, what about us today?

God is just as specific, just as thorough, just as detailed about His temple today—which is us! He said we should separate ourselves and He meant it. He said present yourself as a living sacrifice and He meant it. He said flee from fornication and He meant it.

Do you not know that you are the temple of God and that the Spirit of God dwells in you? (1 Corinthians 3:16, NKJV)

The Scripture says that we are the temple of God. Why didn't the Scripture say that we are the home of God? Why didn't the Spirit say that we are the house of God? Why didn't the Spirit say we are the shelter or the chamber or lodge or camp of God?

Per *Merriam-Webster*, a *house* is where a family lives; a structure or a shelter, and a *temple* is a sanctuary; a house of worship, a place devoted to a special purpose; a place regarded as holy.

Your body is the temple of God; He regarded our bodies as being holy, devoted and designed for a special purpose; your body is regarded as *holy*! GLORY TO THE NAME OF JESUS.

> A temple is like a shrine, a sacred place. It is not only where the Spirit lives, but it is where you worship, honor, and revere our Savior Jesus. That is why it is critical that we conduct ourselves and treat our temple as a place of honor.

A temple is like a shrine, a sacred place. It is not only where the Spirit lives, but it is where you worship, honor, and revere our Savior Jesus. That is why it is critical that we conduct ourselves and treat our temple as a place of honor.

God regards our bodies as sacred, but how do we regard our own bodies? How we behave, how we speak, what we allow into this sacred shrine through our eyes and ears are critically important so that we do *not* defile the temple.

The things we say, the things we do, how we converse with one another, the lack of respect we show one another as children of God—your temple is supposed to be where the HOLIES OF HOLIES dwell. If you evaluate your temple as it stands today, do you think He will be pleased to dwell there? Do not fall out of the will of God. The commandment to bless, and it can't be reversed, is on layaway. Get it off!

If you have no peace, maybe it is because you are defiling the temple. If you have happiness, but no joy, maybe it is because you are defiling your temple. The Bible says the joy of the Lord is your strength; you have no strength because you have no joy; you have temporal happiness because you have corrupted and defiled the temple.

We go through ailments in our bodies, sometimes because we have not regarded it as a sacred shrine. Do you understand the words that are written on these pages? YOU ARE SPECIAL TO GOD! Okay, okay. Let me try to explain it in this regard.

The White House is guarded by the Secret Service. You can only go into the White House by invite. It is guarded day and night.

There are many rooms in this historical monument. People plan vacations, schools plan trips, and tourists travel from around the world to get a glimpse of the outside structure and all of the historical implications it possesses. It is meant to stand as a symbol of democracy and freedom, so it is said.

The White House boasts of 132 rooms, 32 bathrooms, six levels, 412 doors, 147 windows, 28 fireplaces, seven staircases, three elevators, and one inner room or main chamber called the Oval office, which is the office of the U.S. President.

Our bodies are guarded as a temple, a sacred place of worship for the President of our souls. It is guarded by the spiritual secret service, the Holy Spirit. When there is a breach in security (sin), the alarm sounds and a warning is sent. Just as there are secret passages and doorways for the

President and his family to escape in case of an attack, the Spirit provides a way for us to escape a spiritual attack, to prevent the enemy from entering our sacred temple. Isn't that amazing? God regards my body as a place of honor.

1. What do you allow in your temple?
2. Are you cleaning your temple daily with the proper nutrients?
3. Are you taking care of your temple so it retains the beautiful and unique structure that God designed it to have?

I will praise You, for I am fearfully and wonderfully made; marvelous are Your works, and that my soul knows very well. (Psalm 139:14, NKJV)

God desires to be where we are. The question to ask is do we want Him here? You need to talk to your flesh and tell it to sit down and get some business. Ain't nobody got time for these games anymore. We are working on the building, not made by man's hands.

NOTES CHAPTER 15

The Significance of Three

The Father, The Son, The Holy Spirit.

Now so it was that after three days they found Him
in the temple, sitting in the midst of the teachers,
both listening to them and asking them questions.

(Luke 2:46, NKJV)

Jesus, His family, and some friends traveled for a religious ritual called the Feast of the Passover. Here is a little background of what this feast is about. After decades of slavery to the Egyptians, God saw His people's distress, the children of Israel, and sent Moses to Pharaoh with a message: "Let My people go." Despite numerous warnings, Pharaoh refused to listen to God's command. God then sent upon Egypt ten plagues, afflicting them and destroying everything from their livestock to their crops. Basically, God got their attention by hitting them where it hurt most, their pockets. Then, God sent the last of the ten plagues on the Egyptians, killing all their firstborn. But, God spared the children of Israel, "passing over" their homes and that is how the name of the holiday came about: "The feast of the Passover."

And they shall take some of the blood and put it on the two doorposts
and on the lintel of the houses where they eat it. Then they shall eat the
flesh on that night; roasted in fire, with unleavened bread and with bit-
ter herbs they shall eat it. Do not eat it raw, nor boiled at all with water,
but roasted in fire—its head with its legs and its entrails. You shall let
none of it remain until morning, and what remains of it until morning
you shall burn with fire. And thus you shall eat it: with a belt on your
waist, your sandals on your feet, and your staff in your hand. So you
shall eat it in haste. It is the Lord's Passover. For I will pass through the
land of Egypt on that night, and will strike all the firstborn in the land

of Egypt, both man and beast; and against all the gods of Egypt I will execute judgment: I am the Lord. (Exodus 12: 7-12, NKJV)

- Do you have an annual festival of praise to remember what the Lord has done for you?
- Do you remember how He pulled you out of the darkness?
- Do you remember when you called the Lord's name in distress and He answered you?
- Do you remember when you were left for dead, but God said, "NAW NAW, baby, your destiny is in My hands. You WILL live!"

Do you remember?

Back to the subject matter, where we find ourselves back in Luke 2. Jesus was a preteen. The Bible says He was 12 when Jesus and His family traveled this particular year to celebrate the feast of Passover in Jerusalem. When it was time to return home, Jesus was left behind, but Mary and Joseph, His parents, did not know. They assumed Jesus was somewhere in the company with the family and friends that travelled with them.

Let me make this relatable: What had happened was, the Greyhound bus had stopped for a bathroom break when both Mary and Joseph realized that Jesus wasn't playing Uno in the back of the bus with His cousins.

Jesus was back in the city with this religious people of authority. When I read this I wondered:

- Did He stay the entire time in the temple?
- Did He eat? Or was he on a spiritual fast?
- Did He go to the bathroom?
- Did any of the leaders ask where Jesus's parents were?
- If they did, what was Jesus's reply?
- How many questions can He have to spend all day in the temple at age 12?
- Did He miss His parents?
- Did He wonder what they were going to say or how they must have felt not knowing where He was?
- Did He even wonder if they would return for Him?
- Did Jesus think He was gonna be in trouble?
- Did any of the leaders file a missing person report?

The Bible goes on to say Mary, Joseph, and the crew had already been traveling an entire day before realizing Jesus was not with them. They had to travel another day, back to where they had come from. Ooooh weee. My momma would have been frustrated. I don't think I would have gotten off so easy by saying I was about my Father's business. I'm just saying.

When they found young Jesus in the temple:

And it came to pass, that after three days they found him in the temple, sitting in the midst of the doctors, both hearing them, and asking them questions. (Luke 2:46, KJV)

The Importance of THREE

Look at this Scripture (Luke 2:46):

Jesus was sitting.

Jesus was hearing.

Jesus was asking.

When you arrive at the house of God, there are three things you should do.

Sitting

A day in your courts is better than a thousand; I had rather be a door-keeper in the house of MY God than to dwell in the tens of wickedness. (Psalms 84:10)

When we come to the assembly of where God dwells, we are to be seated with anticipation to hear from our father, just like when we sit in anticipation of seeing a good movie, or a sports game or comedy show.

Hearing

So then, faith comes by hearing and hearing by the word of God. (Romans 10:17)

Asking

After you have sat and heard, now it's time to evaluate yourself and ask God to cleanse you from anything that is not like Him. Cleanse your heart. Cleanse your mind, renew your spirit.

Jesus did three things at the age of twelve when He sat in the temple. What are you doing as an adult in the house of God? Let us make sure we have an understanding. Coming to assemble ourselves in the presence of

God isn't done to see who is doing what or who is wearing whatever. I don't go to church to praise and worship my Savior. I do not need church for that. I keep a praise and worship experience going forth in my home, in my car, while I am cooking dinner because the church is in me! Praise is what I do! But when we assemble ourselves together, it is to refuel. It is to hear a word from our Father on how to deal with the nonsense that we face every day. It is to become stronger and stronger in the Spirit of God and to edify one another to remain encouraged. That is why we assemble.

There is something about the importance of the number three. Even the world recognizes the significance of three. It is the Triad, being the number of the whole as it contains the beginning, a middle, and an end. The power of three is universal and is the tripartite nature of the world as heaven, earth, and waters.

Maybe that was too technical. Here are some more common examples of the importance of three:

- I learned early in my elementary education that when I wrote a story, it required three parts: intro, body, and the conclusion.
- In baseball, third base signifies that you're almost home, and three strikes means you are out!
- In basketball, a triangle offense was efficiently used by coach Phil Jackson who led arguably the best player in the NBA, Michael Jordan, to many championships.
- Basketball also operates under a rule called the three-second lane violation.
- In football, a field goal is worth three points.
- In football, the defense may operate a three-man rush. Typically, it's to send the majority of the team down the field to prevent the quarterback from completing a long pass to one of its wide receivers in a desperate move to get back into the game or win the game.

Am I talking right? Now let's see what the Bible says about three:

Though one may be overpowered by another, two can withstand him. And a threefold cord is not quickly broken. (Ecclesiastes 4:12, NKJV)

For where two or three are gathered together in My name, I am there in the midst of them. (Matthew 18:20, NKJV)

And now abide faith, hope, love, these three; but the greatest of these is love. (1 Corinthians 13:13, NKJV)

- Jesus prayed three times in the Garden before His arrest.
- He was placed on the cross at the third hour of the day.
- There were three hours of darkness that covered the land while Jesus was suffering on the cross from the sixth hour to the ninth hour.
- Three is the number of resurrection. Christ was dead for three full days and three full nights.
- The Apostle Paul was caught up to the third heaven. He also was privileged to visit the location of God's throne, which is in the third heavens (2 Corinthians 12:2-4).
- The Bible only mentions the name of three angels, Michael, Gabriel, and Lucifer.
- Jesus is described, in the very beginning of the book of Revelation, as a being "which is, and which was, and which is to come" (Revelation 1:4).
- The ministry of Jesus was three-and-a-half years
- Jesus rose after three days.
- The devil tempted Jesus in the wilderness three times after He fasted 40 days and nights.
- Peter denied Jesus three times.

The importance of three all comes down to this:

For there are three that bear witness in heaven: The Father, the Word, and the Holy Spirit; and these three are one. And there are three that bear witness on earth: The Spirit, the water, and the blood; and these three agree as one. If we receive the witness of men, the witness of God is greater; for this is the witness of God which He has testified of His Son. He who believes in the Son of God has the witness in himself; he who does not believe God has made Him a liar, because he has not believed the testimony that God has given of His Son. And this is the testimony: that God has given us eternal life, and this life is in His Son. 1 John 5:7-11 (NKJV)

Let me break this down!

For there are three that bear record in heaven, the Father, the Word, and the Holy Ghost: and these three are one. (1 John 5:7)

...but this Scripture does not go on to say what the record is.

And there are three that bear witness in earth: The Spirit and the water and the blood; and these three agree in one. (1 John 5:8)

On earth, the Holy Spirit agrees in one with the water and the blood. Again this relates to proof of Jesus' ministry on earth, that He was born in the flesh, that He was baptized, and then He shed His blood on the cross.

If we receive the witness of men, the witness of God is greater: for this is the witness of God which he hath testified of his Son. (1 John 5:9)

This Scripture is saying the witness of the Holy Spirit is greater than the witness of any man.

He that believeth on the Son of God hath the witness in himself. He that believeth not God hath made him a liar; because he believeth not the record that God gave of his Son. (1 John 5:10)

So back in verse 7 we said there are three that bare record in heaven. Here, the word says the record is that God gave His Son, Jesus, but that is not the conclusion of the record.

Here it comes!

And this is the record, that God hath given to us eternal life, and this life is in his Son. (1 John 5:11)

THE RECORD HAS BEEN REVEALED!

The significance of the three is that they work together as a witness on our behalf that we are the children of our Father, and the record is not only here on Earth but also written in heaven. Thank God for a record on earth that Jesus dwelt here in the flesh and left the Holy Spirit to dwell in us, but I need a record in heaven. Are you understanding what I am saying? The record or proof, or report is that the God Head (The Father, The Word, and the Holy Ghost) agree in heaven that we have eternal life in the only begotten son of God. That is so powerful to me. Oh my Savior. And this is why the enemy fights us so hard. It is to negate that record.

Our salvation in the Lord Jesus Christ is secure because the Godhead is in total agreement. He's good with it. God approved it. He agreed to give us eternal life by the works that Jesus had done on earth. Then Jesus, after He had done His work, sent the Holy Spirit to comfort us, to be the spiritually court-appointed stenographer and to be a witness. A witness is a person who is present at an event, who can say it happened. The Holy Spirit can vouch for us.

"Yeah, she was sincere when she came up. Yes, most Holy Father, I was there when he was on his knees crying for Your presence and Your guidance. Yes, Lord, I was there when she was tempted to give in, but she recalled to her mind the joy that You brought her when she surrendered to Your will. Oh, yes, most Holy One, I was there when he was tempted to go OFF, but he quickly remembered that he had asked You to allow his words to always be seasoned with grace and that You set a watch over his mouth so he would not sin against You."

I thank You, Holy Spirit, for Your true witness.

We have inherited eternal life through the repentance of our sins, through our walk with Christ. Let us not become complacent and throw it all away.

SEVENTEEN

My Shut-Up Moment

"I be quiet...but when he leave, I be talking again."

—CHRIS TUCKER

I n the introduction of this book, I expressed how I would share my "shut up and sit down" flesh check. Here it is:

Have you ever experienced something you could not explain, but regardless of what others thought or said, you know what you experienced? Well, I can relate. In the next few moments, I will attempt to share with you something I don't think I'll ever forget. At this juncture in my life, it doesn't matter what others feel, think, or even how they react to what I'm about to share. I do pray and hope that it captures your interest and that you'll pay very close attention to what you do and say for the rest of your life. You ready?

One day after Sunday morning service, I decided to relax, as I often try to do. I was still living at home with my mom and was a recent graduate from college. I love listening to music. It calms me. Music is so powerful—it can set you in a place of negative or positive energy. For example, if you are single and listening to a love song or a song about lost love, if not careful (here comes the flesh!), your mind will drift into the past to relive past relationships. But if you are going through a rough patch in life, I double-dog dare you to put on your favorite praise and worship song. Soon that moment of anxiety will lift and you will feel better about the situation.

On this particular day, I was in a place of meditation. I just wanted to think about the Lord and relax before evening service. Pretty soon, I had unknowingly drifted off. Then my experience began.

Imagine being in a big stadium or some sort of sports complex outside. For example, Lambeau Field, AT&T Stadium, or Mile High Stadium. Picture a stadium filled with people, just talking. You can hear the commotion and a number of conversations going on, but you cannot decipher what the conversations are about. The sun is going down and it is dusk. Suddenly, a sound like that of a siren or bullhorn rings out. The people in the stadium know what that sound means. The conversations end. They all stand up and form a line. It is quiet. Forming a single-file line, they lined behind one another, everyone holding hands while in line. What are they waiting for? They knew they were waiting for their moment.

This is what I saw, but I stood in line, too. Pretty soon, it was my turn to receive what would be placed on my plate. In front of me was a table. On each side of the table was a candle and in between the candles was a book. Behind the table was a huge chair with a high back. I could not see who was sitting in the chair, but it was bright, I mean super bright. Shortly thereafter, I noticed the book was open and the pages are turning, only I am not turning the pages. The pages were moving fast, but not so fast for me to see everything in the pages. As I stood I began to realize that on every page was written everything I ever said or did, from birth until that point of standing before that seat!

Then the book closed. I did not hear a voice, but in the dream, it was like a thought entered my mind and I knew that the Lord was pleased with me up to that point in my life.

Have you ever flown on an airplane? As you approach landing, you can hear the landing gear getting into position. Soon, the wheels hit the pavement, and the brakes are engaged and landing begins. That is what I heard: "Eeeekkkk, boom!" I gasped for breath as I sat up on my bed.

What had just happened? I replayed the entire experience in my head, realizing I had an "out of body" experience. My spirit went to another place and entered back into my body, like a plane landing on a runway.

Can you imagine everything you've done for twenty, thirty, forty, eighty years all recorded on paper? Think about that. This experience happened to me in the spring of 1998 and I will never forget it. Every time I'm dealing with a difficult person or situation, I bring myself back to that moment and remember everything I do and say is being written.

I have come to the conclusion that nothing matters in this life but only to please my Father. I want Him to be proud to call me His daughter. I want Him to say that I carried out the purpose He had for me. I want Him to know and feel that He can depend on me to do what He wants me to do, even when it hurts. I want Him to welcome me in His presence, wrap His arms around me, and never let me go. I cannot experience this if I am not obedient to my Father. Guess what? Neither can you!

I ask you these questions:

1. What is going to keep you accountable?
2. What makes you remain focused on being about the business of our Father?
3. Will God be pleased with what you have said or done up to this point in your life?

Whether you believe or not, life doesn't end after we leave this earth; it begins. It will begin with eternal happiness or eternal damnation. I did not share this most intimate spiritual moment with you to use as a scare tactic, but more so to remind you to consider your actions and intentions.

I was happy to learn I had pleased the Lord up until that point, and that doesn't even matter at this point, because I still have living to do! I have purposed in my heart that I will obey God, through Jesus Christ! What about you? Everything matters.

> *I saw the dead, both great and small, standing before God's throne. And the books were opened, including the Book of Life. And the dead were judged according to what they had done, as recorded in the books. The sea gave up its dead, and death and the grave gave up their dead. And all were judged according to their deeds.* (Revelation 20:12-13, NLT)

Epilogue

The time has come. I have reached the end of my narrative, but not the end of my journey. It is my prayer that you were able to obtain a better understanding about the flesh and the spirit. I would like to conclude with us conversing with our Father so that we may fully open our hearts and minds to receive what the Spirit has to say to us. Please join me in prayer.

Lord, I come to say thank you on today. Thank you for being who you are. Thank you for keeping us sane when insane situations affect our normal routines. In fact, we thank you for the insane situations. For it was through the agony and pain of them that we came to our senses. We recognize that we need you. We cannot navigate through life without you leading us.

Thank you for allowing us to have a place to sleep and a place that we can come together with our families to pronounce as our temporary home, until we return to you. We thank you for making us a vessel of honor for your use and your habitation, as sacred as a temple.

Lord I thank you for bringing value to our lives and exceeding expectations. You gave us worth when others said we were worthless. You cared enough about us to shelter us and cover us in the midst of danger. You dispatched your angels of legal representation to stand with us in courtrooms where we thought we would have to fight alone and you fought on our behalf. You made us valuable. In other words, worth something. Worth means: good, valuable, or important enough for (something); deserving of (something).

After sin entered the world, you said we were important enough to have another chance. After some spoke among themselves about things they understood not, after we brought you to an open shame and impacted others' belief in you because we did not represent who you are, after day in and day out of performing the ritual of going to church services and not applying what we were hearing, after blaming you for the bad things, disrespecting you but then having the audacity to request the "good things" from you...You gave us worth.

You thought we deserved to inherit eternal life. You thought we deserved to have your precious Spirit dwell within us. You thought we deserved to have our sins forgiven and to be cleansed by the blood of the Lamb, Jesus Christ. You thought we deserved to have some small impartation of your amazing gifts in us, to display among others, but all to uplift and glorify you.

You thought we deserved to carry the mantle of your word that cleanses the heart, soothes the soul, and strengthens the feeble minded. You thought we deserved to allow your only child to give His life as a sacrifice so that we could live. That leaves me speechless.

You thought...that we...deserved You!

(Here come the tears). Lord, I love You today and every day. I simply cannot thank You enough. Even with bad news, You can make it good. I love You beyond the words that I can speak or write.

YOU THOUGHT WE DESERVED YOU!

Praise Your name, Jesus. I humbly ask that You accept this prayer. In Jesus's name, amen.

"You thought I was worth saving, so you came and changed my life. You thought I was worth keeping, so you cleaned me up inside. You thought I was to die for, so you sacrificed your life. So I could be free, so I could be whole, so I could tell everyone I know."
—ANTHONY BROWN AND GROUP THERAPY

Acknowledgements

I would like to take this moment to thank everyone who has embraced me in some capacity or another. Whether that was an encouraging word through ministering in the pulpit, text, social media, my devotion app, in person, or through an exchange of hugs, thank you.

Thank you to Rhonda Ware for pushing me, my husband for always believing in me and helping me to walk in the measure of grace that has been given to me. Thank you to my children for putting up with my attitudes and emotional rollercoaster, when I was focused on completing this assignment. Even when I'm not on assignment, Dad is always there to say, "Come on! You know how your mother is." Yep, I hear him when I'm in another room. LOL.

Thank you to my mother for stepping in when and where we needed. Thanks to Money Graphics, Newleaf Design for lending your gifts to my vision and your willingness to meet some of my short timelines and targeted dates with design and layout.

Anything that I have shared on this topic of flesh and spirit has been a result of my own struggles, ah-ha moments, and disappointments. Through it all, I continue to learn more about the separation of flesh and spirit so that I can, as the old hymn would say, draw nearer my God to thee.

About Kimberly

The Life

After graduating from high school at the age of 16, the University of Wisconsin- Milwaukee welcomed Kim as a student to pursue a Bachelor's Degree in Management Information Systems. Later, upon taking a year off, she completed her Master's Degree in Telecommunications at Keller Graduate School of Management in June 2002.

The Writer

In August 2002, Kimberly Lock married the love of her life, Marlon Lock. They have four daughters and a son. Kimberly has built a spiritual atmosphere in her home, where she balances the delicate tasks of nurturing and guiding her children, handling the business aspects of the church her husband pastor's, Unity Gospel House of Prayer in Milwaukee, WI., managing her husband's music career, and pursuing her endeavors has an author and speaker.

Kimberly never desired to write in any capacity. Her personal desires have always been centered around technology – building and configuring servers. However, she learned of her purpose – when life took an unexpected turn through ministry. Kimberly's passion is to empower women and for them to recognize who defines their value and worth. Her first book was written for women to recognize their worth through eyes of God. *Who You Callin' Silly?: How a Silly Woman Becomes Virtuous* was released June 2012. While that book was in print, the Lord gave her a vivid dream regarding a children's series with the titles, direction, packaging and purpose.

In 2015, the "The Disregarded Voice of a Child" (aka The Mommy Series) was completed through self-publication, but had gone through many roadblocks with publishing and distribution. After moving from self-publishing to receiving a publishing contract for the children's series, Kimberly began focusing her efforts on children. While planning to market and release her children's series, a since of urgency was impressed upon Kimberly to write a book that focuses more on spiritual mind renewal.

In 2016, Kimberly Lock made the tough decision to temporarily table the children's series and complete her new book: *Shut Up and Sit Down: A*

Candid Conversation with the Flesh. Sharing her own personal experiences, Kimberly gives readers a vivid picture of how the flesh and spirit are in constant war with one another, with the objective of the flesh being to destroy us.

One of Kimberly's mentors impressed upon her to launch her own publishing company. Uncertain if she was truly hearing God's voice, the same day Kimberly learned the publishing company, who had offered an unbelievable deal for her children's series, was no longer publishing and would offer its existing authors full rights to all material. Kimberly moved expeditiously and carefully to create KRL Publishing.

The Speaker

Kimberly assists her husband in the business aspects of their church, Unity Gospel House of Prayer, Milwaukee Wisconsin. She also facilitates a bi-monthly forum entitled: "Talk Time w/Lady Kimberly Lock" at the church, where women discuss issues of life and how to mitigate those issues through the Word of God. She has also been given the opportunity to speak at various women's conferences and on radio stations.

You're invited to connect with author at:
www.shutupandsitdownbook.com
Facebook: Author Kimberly Lock
Instagram/Twitter: @AuthorKimLock

CPSIA information can be obtained
at www.ICGtesting.com
Printed in the USA
LVHW092152020419
612770LV00001B/57/P